3488 HYDRO INTERNATIONAL

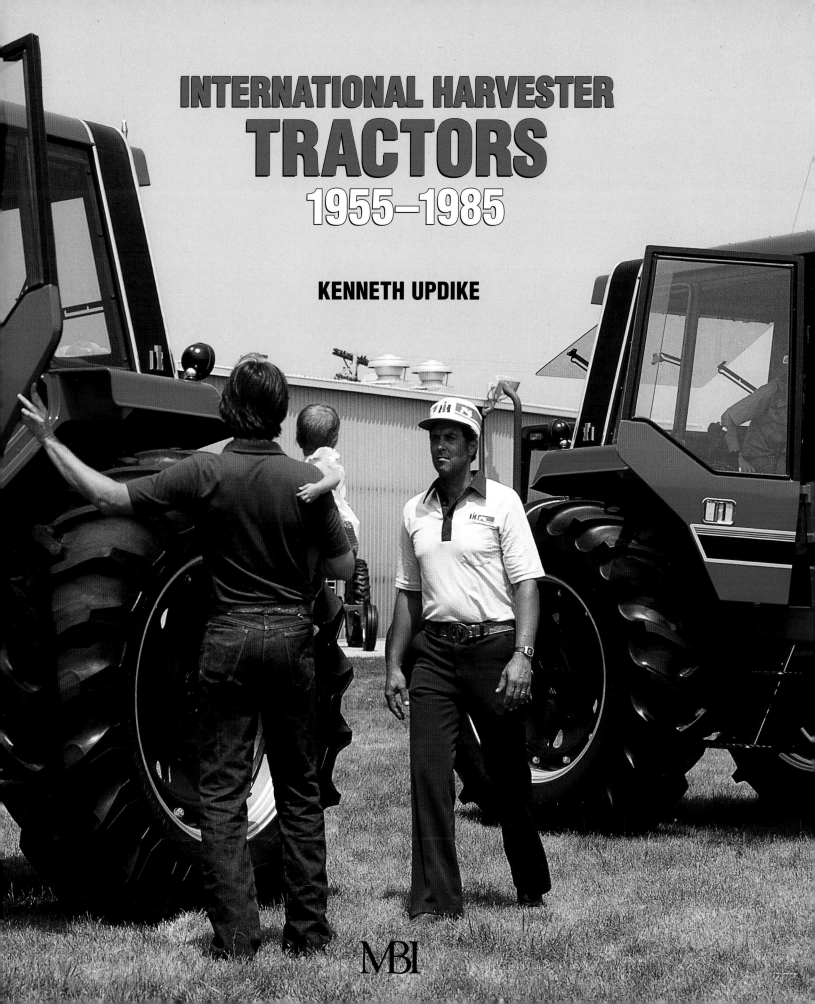

INTERNATIONAL HARVESTER
TRACTORS
1955–1985

KENNETH UPDIKE

MBI

This edition first published in 2000 by MBI, an imprint of MBI Publishing Company, Galtier Plaza, Suite 200, 380 Jackson Street, St. Paul, MN 55101-3885 USA

The information in this book is true and complete to the best of our knowledge. All recommendations are made without any guarantee on the part of the author or Publisher, who also disclaim any liability incurred in connection with the use of this data or specific details.

This publication has not been prepared, approved, or licensed by International Harvester. We recognize, futher that some words, model names, and designations mentioned herein are the property of the trademark holder. We use them for identification purposes only. This is not an official publication.

MBI titles are also available at discounts in bulk quantity for industrial or sales-promotional use. For details write to Special Sales Manager at MBI Publishing Company, Galtier Plaza, Suite 200, 380 Jackson Street, St. Paul, MN 55101-3885 USA

Library of Congress
Cataloging-in-Publication Data
Updike, Kenneth
    International Harvester tractors
1955–1985 / Kenneth Updike.
        p. cm.
    Includes index.
    ISBN-13: 978-0-7603-0682-6
    ISBN-10: 0-7603-0682-6 (hc. : alk.)
    1. IHC tractors—History. I. Title.
TL233.6.138 U63 2000
    629.225'2'0973—dc21   99-086228

On the front cover: IH's replacement for the Farmall M was the 400. The 400 incorporated IH's new "Fast Hitch" implement hitching system. This 400 is shown pulling a mounted IH Fast Hitch plow. *Author Collection*

On the frontispiece: IH dealers have always offered genuine service replacement parts and factory-trained servicemen to keep IH products up and running. *Author Collection*

On the title page: It seems that the whole family is going to the IH dealer to check out the new 3488 Hydro. Why not? The 3488 Hydro offered smooth one-lever speed and directional control. A deluxe cab with heater and air conditioner make the long days of field work seem much shorter. *Author Collection*

On the back cover: The twin exhaust stacks are characteristic of the 145-horsepower 1468 V-8 diesel tractor. Built from 1971 through 1974, the 1468 was the talk of the neighborhood. *Author Collection*

Edited by Keith Mathiowetz
Designed by Laura Henrichsen

Printed in Hong Kong

Contents

Acknowledgments   *6*

Preface   *7*

Chapter 1   *The 1950s*
From Letters to Numbers   *9*

Chapter 2   *The 1960s*
Six-Cylinder Horsepower
Dominates the Marketplace   *31*

Chapter 3   *The 1970s*
Power and Comfort Are Redefined   *63*

Chapter 4   *The 1980s*
End of an Era   *109*

Index   *128*

Preface

The 1950s saw the increase in tractor horsepower continuing to climb. Postwar advances in hydraulics and machine technology helped International Harvester improve its designs. The fiasco of the 460–560 series was caused by IH management's simple arrogance of thinking, "If we build it, they will buy." This did not work and IH paid the price with lost sales and longtime loyal customers who switched colors.

When IH introduced the 06 series in 1963, it made a major step in the right direction. A light of hope flared brightly. The introduction of the 656 Hydro was a tractor millennium milestone. No other manufacturer had ever tried this type of drivetrain in a commercial tractor. Ironically, with all of the power-shift transmission tractors made today, manufacturers still want to emulate the Hydro's performance.

In the 1970s, IH introduced greater operator comfort with the new 86 series. A greatly improved cab was the main feature, but the tractor still lacked a power-shift transmission. At the end of the 1970s, IH's new 2+2 tractor was pure innovation. It caught the competition by complete surprise, and led to the small row-crop four-wheel drives that are so popular today.

When the farm economy "went south" in the 1980s, IH was in for the ride of its life. It would not emerge from the storm that swept America's heartland. The 50 series tractors were released too late to help the company. If only IH had had them out in 1976, it might have weathered the storm. Eventually, IH sold its ag unit off, to be merged with J. I. Case Co.

Despite this unhappy ending, the development of farm tractor breakthroughs by IH was steady, even after the 1950s. Many of the tractor designs the company developed are seen in the machines of today. This book will explore a number of them.

Acknowledgments

*T*he research and production of this book would not be possible without the help of many others. To list them in any kind of order would be entirely unfair, so I'll do my best from memory.

Thank you, Guy Fay; without your research and sharing of information, this project would have stopped in its tracks long ago. The trips we make to the "vault" at Hinsdale are always eye- and mind-opening. I can't express my thanks to Guy enough for all of his efforts in telling and preserving IH's great past. I must admit that this project came about as a deal I seem to have with Guy. He does IH books from the 1950s back; I want to do them from 1950 on. He steered me to MBI Publishing Company.

Thank you, Lee Klancher, my editor for this project at MBI Publishing Company. I really believe that this could not have happened without your help.

A special thanks to everyone at the State Historical Society of Wisconsin. My near-last-minute photo order was stressful for me. Without the historical society's great care of priceless IH materials, this book would not be possible. How can you decide which "bad" photos of IHs don't make the cut? They are all great!

Thanks to Rich Seraga, Alan Leupold, and Jeff Powell, all of whom work at the Case-IH (Hinsdale, Illinois) Engineering Center. The immeasurable research tips and "found" prints of old IHs are well appreciated. The extra fact checking and printmaking by Jeff is itself worthy of dinner at the Machine Shed. Thanks!

Thank you to my employer, Carter & Gruenewald Co., Inc., the IH dealers in Brooklyn and Juda, Wisconsin. My thanks to them for allowing me to leave my "real" job to go on day trips to Hinsdale, Racine, or the IH Archives to work at my "other" job. The knowledge I have gained from working there through the parts department and our Internet site (www.cngco.com) is invaluable.

Special thanks go to Lowell Kittleson, one of the salesmen at the Brooklyn, Wisconsin, dealer. Lowell, a former IH service rep and former IH dealer, is a walking computer on IH machinery—especially diesel tractor–pulling engines. His allowing me to tap his brain for tips on my 1206 and 806 restorations is deeply appreciated. With Lowell, I quickly gained confidence in my ability to repair the Rosa Master injection pump on my 1206. He dumped all the pump parts on the workbench and said, "Here you go, put it back." Of course, under his watchful eye, I mastered the pump, even getting the 1206 to start on its first try. The experience this man has with IH equipment cannot be described—especially when tractor pulling is involved. He has "been there and done that."

I also want to thank the late Everett Boston, who gave me real world experience with IH machinery. His love of IH ran as deep as mine. His fanatical maintenance records and clean line of IH machinery made him the envy of many farmers. Even though you are not with us any more, I still remember.

This book would not even have been thought of had it not been for my grandparents being lifelong farmers. The many winters spent helping haul firewood with the H or field work with the M are permanently etched in my mind. Everything on their farm was IH (except a feed hammer mill). My early exposure to RED has caused this "sickness" that I have, this IH fever.

Finally, a big thanks to my wife, Charlene. She has the sanity to pull me away from the computer when it is 11 p.m. and I just got another great IH flash. This book project was delayed a month or two so we could get married. All of the late nights spent at the computer have also allowed me to observe our cat. What a life she has. I took a few self-induced cat naps (at the computer) myself before this book was done.

Chapter 1

The 1950s

FROM LETTERS TO NUMBERS

*I*nternational Harvester's New Numbered series—100 through 600 IH Tractors—was introduced in 1955. Also in that year, IH replaced its "lettered" series of tractors (Super A through Super W9) with newly restyled numbered tractors—the 100 through 600 models. The Super A-1 became the model 100, the Super C was now the 200, the Super H became the 300, and the Super MTA was now the 400.

IH did plan to build a Super HTA model and had even authorized its production. The release of the 300 tractor for production, however, overtook the Super HTA development. It's very doubtful if the Super HTA ever got past the prototypical model stage.

The 300 and 400 now had sleek, streamlined hoods that narrowed at the operator's platform for outstanding forward visibility. Highly polished stainless-steel emblems gleamed against the IH red paint. IH used these metal emblems to identify the tractor's name and model number. This use of metal plates continued until the 66 series was introduced in the 1970s. The basic tractor control layout was similar to the previous Super series except that now the tractor had an actual instrument panel at the operator station. By the operator simply turning a key and then

pushing a button, the tractor would come to life. No more pulling wire rods or stepping on switch buttons to start the machine. An engine-mounted mechanical drive hour meter was an available option. For those tractors equipped with battery ignition, a combination speedometer, tachometer, and hour meter was offered as an attachment. With these, the operator could look below the instrument panel and check both the engine and tractor speeds. The hour meter provided a means to record hours of engine operation for maintenance purposes. Power steering was an optional attachment for added operator comfort. With these models, a hydraulic power assist unit was located between the steering wheel and the front bolster. The Behlen Mfg. Co. built this attachment unit for IH. The hydraulic power was supplied from the engine-driven hydraulic pump.

The advances in tractor hydraulics were quickly progressing, and their uses were too. The new hydraulic system on the 300 and 400 was called the "Touch Control" system. International Harvester had also used this name on the previous model Super C and Super A tractors. To operate the Touch Control hydraulics, the operator moved one of either two or three levers. Tractors with

A Farmall 140 equipped with a one-row Fast Hitch–mounted middle buster. The live hydraulic system on the 140 was made possible by using an engine-driven hydraulic pump. The hydraulic system not only operated the Fast Hitch, but had capabilities of powering remote implement-mounted cylinders too. *Author Collection*

The new fleet of Farmall tractors for 1955. Shown (L-R) is the Farmall 400, Farmall 300, Farmall 200, Farmall 100, and Farmall Cub. Notice that the 200, 300, and 400 have the optional front wheel ballast weights added. This indicates that the tractor is equipped with the IH Fast Hitch rear implement hitching system. The Cub and 100 shown here are also equipped with the Fast Hitch. *State Historical Society of Wisconsin*

two levers had only auxiliary tractor hydraulics. With three-lever models, the third lever controlled the tractor's hydraulically operated rear hitch, which IH designated the "Fast Hitch."

The introduction of the new 00 series also brought a new naming system to the IH tractor line. The Farmall model now described the row-crop version of a particular tractor. The International model designated the standard tread and utility-style tractors. The introduction of the Utility tractor was a new feature of the 00 series. This model was similar in

appearance to the International tractor, but offered adjustable wheel-tread settings. IH named its first utility-style tractor the International 300 Utility. The I-300 (as it was called) offered the same engines and transmission choices as the F-300 did, but had a lower height profile. Underslung exhaust was standard on the I-300. IH Fast Hitch, TA (planetary gear reduction unit), and independent PTO were optional. The choices of gasoline, diesel, or LPG engines—just like those in the Farmall series—were also available. The lower height of the Utility models

made them ideal for front-end loaders, and accessing lower-roofed buildings where a Farmall could not go.

The 300 tractor was available in both Farmall and International Utility versions. During the 1954–1956 production run, the 300 became the first IH tractor whose Utility model was produced in greater numbers than its Farmall model. IH manufactured 30,851 I-300s compared to 29,077 Farmall tractors—close, but a sign of things to follow. Both versions of the 300 used an IH-built four-cylinder C-

IH's replacement for the famous Super MTA was its new 50-horsepower model called the 400. This view clearly shows the three levers beside the dash used to operate the Touch Control hydraulic system. This gave the tractor a smoother, cleaner appearance. The rear-mounted Fast Hitch is also shown in the photo. *State Historical Society of Wisconsin*

Nebraska Tractor Tests: 1955 and 1956

Model	Fuel	Test No.	Belt HP
Farmall 400	Gasoline	532	50.78
W-400	Gasoline	533	51.94
Farmall 400	Diesel	534	46.73
W-400	Diesel	535	46.61
Farmall 100	Gasoline	537	20.13
Farmall 300	Gasoline	538	38.16
I-300 Utility	Gasoline	539	41.26
Farmall 400	LPG	571	52.36
W-400	LPG	572	50.72
Farmall 300	LPG	573	38.42
I-300 Utility	LPG	574	42.68

169 gasoline engine that delivered 38 PTO horsepower. The IH Fast Hitch was an available option on both models, as was the IH Torque Amplifier. One very important fact about the I-300 is that tractor SN#501 was also the 3 millionth IH-built tractor. This landmark tractor was built April 5, 1955, at the Farmall Works in Rock Island, Illinois.

The model 400 tractor replaced the revered Super MTA in 1955. The W-400 replaced the Super W-6TA. The Standard tread model of the 400 was still called the "W" series, and not re-named the "I" series as the 300 was. The 400 offered the operator a true instrument panel dash, just as the 300 had. The 400 was offered in gasoline-, diesel-, and LPG-powered versions. The company also built a Hi-Clearance model. IH built 38,360 tractors in its 1955–1957 production run. One of the new features of the 400 was the rear Fast Hitch option. Using this, the operator could back up to the implement, lift, and go!

Operator comfort was improved by IH with the addition of a small backrest being added to a new pan-type seat.

The IH Torque Amplifier . . . TA

With its introduction of the Super MTA tractor, IH now had a partial power-shift tractor transmission. Instead of being limited to 5 forward speeds, the operator had 10 speeds available. Speed selection was better, due to the Torque Ampflier. The TA, as it was commonly called, was a planetary gear reduction unit, often referred to as a mechanical TA, because the clutch is mechanically engaged. This unit was located in the housing between the engine and the transmission gears—known as the clutch housing—on tractors up to the 660, or the speed housing on the 706 and later IH tractors. IH continued to use the mechanical TA in tractors having up to 70 horsepower into 1980, with the last IH tractor using this type of TA being the model 686.

The TA allowed operation in either regular (direct) drive from the en-

County fairs are one of the best places to show farm machinery to farmers. IH was very aggressive at this, and this 1956 photo shows the IH lineup at such an event. Combines, crawlers, implements, and tractors are all on display here. Take special notice of the W-400 in the foreground that is pulling an IH hay baler and has the rare IH Electrall option on it. *State Historical Society of Wisconsin*

gine to the transmission or with a reduced-gear drive ratio of 1.482 to 1. When in TA the travel speed was reduced 32 percent and the pulling ability increased 48 percent. This gear reduction is accomplished by transmitting engine power to a primary and secondary sun gear and three compound planet gears. This unit is controlled by a spring-loaded clutch operated via a hand lever.

When the unit is in Direct Drive (with the control lever forward), the TA clutch is engaged, causing the primary sun gear and planet carrier to turn as a unit. The primary sun gear and compound planet gears cannot turn in relation to each other. This causes the secondary sun gear to turn at the same rate of speed. The secondary sun gear, belt pulley, and transmission driving gear all turn together.

If the control lever is pulled back, the TA clutch is released. Now the planet carrier no longer turns with the primary sun gear and shaft. The gear reduction of the sun and planet gears tends to reverse the rotation of the planet carrier. To prevent this, an overrunning clutch is used. This overrunning clutch will allow the carrier to turn freely in the engine's rotational direction, but holds the unit stationary when it tries to turn in the opposite direction. Now that the carrier is being held still, the sun gear turns the compound planet gear shafts. Use of two different-sized gears on the planet shafts provides double gear reduction. The secondary sun gear now turns the belt pulley and transmission driving gear at a slower speed.

The TA offers the operator a chance to reduce tractor speed while increasing pull power without clutching! The TA can only offer engine-braking transmission if the lever is in the forward (direct) position. If the lever is in the TA position, a downhill runaway could occur. The operator's manual specifically states that the TA lever must be in the forward position under the following circumstances:

When necessary to tow or push the tractor to start the engine.

When operating the side-mounted belt pulley to obtain normal belt speeds.

A studio shot of a plain Farmall 400 that is lacking any options. Missing are rear fenders, front frame weights, Fast Hitch rear hitching system, and power adjustable rear wheels. This tractor would be ideally equipped either for a price conscious buyer or for using with a mounted two-row corn picker. *State Historical Society of Wisconsin*

The manual also states never to move the lever while traveling downhill from Direct Drive to the TA position. Overspeeding of the TA can occur causing the TA to possibly disintegrate and resulting in loss of operator control. The author knows of several instances where this has occurred. One involved a tractor and a loaded grain wagon. In this instance, the driver gained too much speed going downhill and pulled the TA lever back for engine braking. The TA exploded, causing the planet gears to exit the carrier and punch their way through the gas tank. Luckily, the driver survived unhurt. The tractor and wagon did not.

The IH "Fast Hitch" Concept

The IH "Fast Hitch" was first unveiled in the model Super C tractor.

This unique rear implement attaching system was just what the name said: Fast Hitch. The implement's specially mounted tabs allowed the operator to back up to it, latch the hooks into the receiver sockets on the tractor, and then go. No pins, chains, or clevises to use or lose. The operator never left the seat. This was a fast and safe method of implement hookup.

The Ford tractor had a rear hitching system called a three-point hitch that it had licensed from Harry Ferguson. IH engineers studied this hitch and discovered its strengths and weaknesses. To get around any patent problems, IH developed its own rear-implement hitching system called the Fast Hitch. This was similar to the three-point hitch, in that it used two lower lift arms to attach the implement to the tractor. The three-point hitch later became the industry standard, not because it was better, but because IH refused to license its Fast Hitch design to other tractor manufacturers.

IH built two different-sized Fast Hitches. The larger model fit the 300 and 400. The smaller model fit the 100 and 200. The physical width of the mounting tongs was identical for both sizes; the height or thickness of the tongs was the variable. The Fast Hitch on the 100–200 used a thinner tong. Implements for a 100–200 could be used on the 300–400 if special filler plates were added to the hitching sockets. Implements designed for the 300–400 would not fit the 100–200. IH did not recommend using the little tractor implements on the bigger tractors "unless specifically recommended by IH," as

overpowering, and consequent breakage or damage would occur.

The IH Fast Hitch offered the operator a choice of settings to get the exact job done correctly. The Fast Hitch could be adjusted for free floating or rigid implement action vertically, horizontally, or diagonally. A hydraulic cylinder controlled the depth adjustment and implement raising/lowering. Moving a single console-mounted lever operated this cylinder. The hitch was leveled manually by rotating a hand-crank adjusting screw.

The other feature was called "Traction Control." This allowed the operator to move a lever to change the amount of ground pressure on the rear tires, with a choice of four different settings. This was a mechanically operated

system that solved the erratic draft control of the competitive three-point hitch system. By using a mechanical linkage system, the implement draft load caused the cylinder to move the hitch rockshaft upward. When this reaction happened, weight was transferred to the rear wheels. As the draft load increased, so did the amount of weight transferred to the wheels. This reduced wheel slippage. One of the features of Traction Control was the ability of the tractor to keep the implement in the ground, even if it traveled over a field terrace or other irregularity in the field. No tools were needed to make changes; a simple handle just needed moving.

IH had experimented with a rear hitching system in the 1940s called the "Frame-All." IH needed a rear-implement hitching system that was easy to use but that had a reliable draft-control system. They also needed a hitch to get around any patent infringements on the Ferguson three-point hitch. After a few years of testing, the Frame-All design was abandoned. Today, only one example of this prototype tractor is believed to have survived.

The IH Electrall "Shocks the World"

Another IH innovation that never caught on because it was too advanced for its time was called the "Electrall." The Electrall was a large electric generator mounted on the tractor in the location where the belt pulley normally would be—but only on tractors equipped with independent power take-off (PTO) drive. The generator converted the mechanical energy of the tractor into electrical energy that could be used for a wide variety of farm tasks. A remote-mounted electric motor (instead of the tractor's PTO) on a baler or combine, for example, was just one of the many uses of the Electrall. The Electrall could also be used as a standby generator in emergency power outages.

The generator produced alternating current power at 60 cycles. This was identical to that used on farm-

Cleaning up around the farmstead is a never-ending task. Here a Cub Lo-Boy tractor outfitted with a front-mounted IH grading blade makes quick work of moving fence-row debris. The hydraulic implement lift feature on the tractor makes raising/lowering the blade easy. *State Historical Society of Wisconsin*

IH gave its tractor lineup an overhaul in 1957 with the introduction of a new two-tone red/white paint scheme. Shown here (L-R) are the new Cub, 130 (which replaced the 100), 230 (which replaced the 200); and the 350 and 450, replacements for the 300 and 400. The basic tractors remained the same, but the new paint helped to boost sales. *State Historical Society of Wisconsin*

steads across the United States. The Electrall had a 37.5-amp capacity and was made by General Electric for IH. It was also offered in a trailer-mounted version. This was powered by the tractor's PTO power, leaving the belt pulley free for operation too.

IH considered the Electrall a safer alternative to the PTO shaft implement drives, which were not then considered dangerous but, IH believed, could possibly prove fatal. With the shaft style, the possibility of injury or entanglement was very high, especially if proper shielding was missing. With only electrical cords available at the time to transmit power, IH felt the Electrall offered a huge safety advantage over the shaft drives. The Electrall never took off in sales despite International Harvester's valiant marketing effort. Farmers

This Farmall 450, equipped with a Fast Hitch rear-mounted plow, is plowing some winter wheat. This 450 is equipped not only with the optional Fast Hitch, but has both front frame weights and wheel weights along with power adjusted rear tread wheels. *State Historical Society of Wisconsin*

It's chore time in the stockyard, and that means loading manure with an IH power loader into a waiting IH spreader being pulled by a Farmall 350. Loading tasks were made easier with advances in tractor hydraulics that IH used. *State Historical Society of Wisconsin*

A wide front-end Farmall 450 pulls an IH beet harvester in this field of sugar beets. Once a labor-intensive operation, beet harvesting became highly mechanized with the invention of mechanical harvesters. IH offered beet harvesting machinery through the late 1960s. *State Historical Society of Wisconsin*

seemed to prefer the use of PTO shaft-driven implements instead.

"Refinement" of the Old: The 130–650 Series Tractors

Two years after the release of the "00" series tractors, IH upgraded them to the "50" series of tractors. The 300 became the 350; and the 400, the 450. The smaller tractors were changed to the "30" series. The 100 became the 130; and the 200, the 230.

Basically the tractors remained unchanged, except that all models now sported a two-color paint scheme of IH red with a white grille and white hood panel accent area. Actually, the only white-painted area was the grille. The white areas on the side hood panels are decals, not painted!

The other major change was to the Fast Hitch. IH added two features to this. One was called "Pilot Guide" control, a device that looked like a thermometer, located on the left side of the tractor dash. With Pilot Guide, the tractor operator could look forward and watch the indicator, instead of turning back to watch the implement. By comparing the reading on the implement depth indicator to the operator's preset depth, the implement could be raised or lowered for even depth tillage.

In the spring of 1957, IH released for production the new model 330 Utility tractor.

The 330 was built only as a utility, never as a Farmall. IH installed in it the newly designed, IH-built C-135 four-cylinder engine, which had been designated for the 340 tractor, even though the 340, whose design was still unfinished, didn't even exist yet! Rather than let the tooling lie idle, however, the company decided to mate the new C-135 with an I-350 tractor, and the I-330 was born. With a list price of around $2,800, the I-330 actually cost less than the I-350.

The IH 350 tractor was offered with gasoline-, LPG-, and diesel-engine choices. The really unique twist to this was that the diesel engine was not an IH! It was a Continental! IH had a four-cylinder diesel engine in development, but it was not ready for production yet. Continental made a long line of engines used by other tractor manufacturers. IH was always one to use its own if possible, but it needed a diesel model in this class to meet the competition.

IH had the Cub retested at Nebraska because the engine rpm had increased from 1,600 to 1,800 rpm. This resulted in a new belt horsepower rating of 10.39, versus the previous rating of 9.23 horsepower.

The model 450 was basically unchanged from the prior model 400. The optional factory-installed power steering system was a choice that few farmers opted for. The basic drivetrain and options were similar to the 400. One new option was the choice of power-adjusted rear wheels. Allis-Chalmers had used this style of wheel for years on its WD and WD-45 models to get all rear tread adjustment, because of those models' flange hub axle design. IH built 25,565 Farmall versions, and another 1,974 W-450 Internationals.

One of the bigger complaints IH received on the new numbered tractors was that they were "gas hogs." Farmers who had bought a 00 series tractor said the new models consumed a lot more fuel than the older, letter series tractors did. It seemed like less work could be done on a tank of fuel. Actually, this was an illusion. The Farmall M had a 21-gallon fuel tank. The Farmall 400 could have either a 21-gallon or an 18-gallon tank. If the farmer had traded a Farmall M for a Farmall 400 with an 18-gallon tank, it would obviously do less work on a tank of fuel.

"Getting Down to Brass Tacks": The 450 "Brass Tacks" Demonstrator Program

IH had long been a company that marketed its line through farm demonstrations. When the IH 350 and 450 tractors came out, the company had a special demo program, which it called the "Brass Tacks" tractor demo program. IH would send a specially decaled tractor from its factory to its dealers, who were instructed to point out its unique

Nebraska Tractor Tests: 1954–1957			
Model	Fuel	Test No.	Belt HP
Farmall 130	Gasoline	617	22.23
Farmall 230	Gasoline	616	28.06
Farmall 350	Gasoline	611	40.71
Farmall 350	Diesel	609	38.65
Farmall 350	LPG	622	41.53
Farmall 450	Gasoline	612	55.28
Farmall 450	Diesel	608	48.78
Farmall 450	LPG	620	54.12
I-350 Utility	Gasoline	615	43.32
I-350 Utility	Diesel	610	42.89
I-350 Utility	LPG	619	45.24
I-650	Gasoline	618	62.11
I-650	LPG	621	63.91
W-450	Gasoline	533	51.94
W-450	LPG	572	50.72
W-450	Diesel	535	46.61

features. The dealer would then take the tractor to as many farmers as possible to try out on their farms. After the demo program had ended or the tractor had a minimum of 100 demo hours (within a time period of eight months from tractor invoice date), the dealer could sell it. A dealer could also use a tractor from his own stock for a demo tractor, if it met the attachment option and time

This operator seems to enjoy "making hay" and why not? With a Farmall Cub and side-mounted sickle bar mower, this job gets done fast! The unique "offset" seat design of the Cub offers unparalleled vision for the operator. *State Historical Society of Wisconsin*

With an IH four-bottom moldboard plow in tow, this Farmall 450 gasoline-powered tractor is making quick work of this field of sod. At the touch of a fingertip, the driver can move a lever actuating the tractor's remote hydraulic valve and lifting the plow. The days of using a trip rope were disappearing; hydraulics had replaced mechanical lifts. *Author Collection*

Raking hay is easy when you have a Farmall 140 tractor teamed with a McCormick five-bar side delivery rake. The wide padded seat and "offset" design of the 140 give the driver more comfort and better visibility. After this hay dries, it will be baled and stored inside the large white barn in the background, the dairy barn used by IH at its Hinsdale, Illinois, experimental farm. *Author Collection*

criteria set forth by IH. The company offered a dealer-installed tractor demo decal kit.

The demo program was successful in that it did help IH sell tractors, but many dealers also used this opportunity to sell the entire line of IH implements to the farmer at the same time. Often, many IH plows, harrows, and hay machines were sold instead of tractors. Sometimes the farmer didn't like or need a new tractor, but a new plow or disk harrow could be much more affordable. IH gained sales of machinery from a tractor demo program. That is pretty good cross-marketing.

The theme IH used for this was called the "Brass Tacks" tractor demo. When an event was held, the dealer would hand out small brass tacks to the participants, signifying that they had witnessed a demo. The term Brass Tacks was a reference to the turn-of-the-century phrase that meant getting down to the basics or the details of an item. IH

was quick to capitalize on the advantages its tractors had over the competition and used this to help sell IH tractors. An interesting note is that the Brass Tacks demo program was held during the middle of the 450 tractor's production life. IH did this for one reason, to pump new sales life into an "old" product. Whenever a new tractor series is announced, sales take off. Later, after the tractors have been on the market for a while, they seemed to lose their "new shine" appeal. Any way of drawing attention to your product certainly helps, and that was the purpose of the demo program. Finding an original IH Brass Tacks 450 demo tractor today would be very rare good fortune.

Little Tractors With a New Look

The new model 140 tractor (which replaced the previous model 130) was released for production in a Farm Tractor Engineering Department Special Notice and Change Letter dated December

20, 1956. In this letter, IH specifies that the new 140 Farmall and 140 Hi-Clearance tractors would have the following basic features: A new C-123 gasoline engine that uses a single belt to power the water pump, fan, and generator. A new radiator and radiator grille support. A new 12-volt electrical system. And finally, new sheet-metal styling to match the rest of the newly announced tractor series. All of these changes were to go into effect in November of 1957.

A "new" Farmall Cub and International Cub Lo-Boy tractors were also released for production in a special change letter dated January 24, 1957. In this note, IH states that the tractors will remain the same as previous models except with the following changes: A new friction-type governor control, a 12-volt electrical system, and a new radiator grille and grille supports for the revised styling changes. These new Cub tractors were due out in November of 1957 too.

The Farmall 240 replaced the model 230 tractor. Once again the major change was new sheet-metal styling to match the rest of the series. The 240 was offered in both Farmall and International Utility styles. IH used Farmall 240 SN#505 as its Nebraska test model; it recorded 30.99 maximum horsepower. Using an IH-built four-cylinder gasoline engine with a displacement of 123 ci, the Farmall 240 was the top two- to three-plow tractor in maximum drawbar pounds pull. The John Deere 420 was rated at 3,790 pounds and the Ford 641 at 3,054 pounds. Compare this to the Farmall 240's 4,343-pound rating, and it's easy to see who really was "king of the hill." The Farmall 240 also topped the competition in four out of five fuel-economy tests. Even with this extra brawn (the 240 weighed 500 pounds more than the Ford 641) and great fuel economy, the 240 was still cost comparable to the Deere and Ford. The Farmall 240 had a list price of $2,530.66.

The next addition to the IH line of Utility tractors was the I-240. Using the basic power train and engine from the I-240, along with a lower wide front axle and smaller diameter rear wheels, this

In this photo, dated 1956, IH is attempting to show the soon-to-be-released model 240. The tractor is labeled as a model 200 (the current production model at the time). The underslung exhaust system is unique in its pipe routing, as are the clamshell-style rear fenders. Neither of these made it into final production. The battery is still located ahead of the shifting lever, making entry and egress difficult at best. *State Historical Society of Wisconsin*

proved that it "had the right stuff" to be used in both farm and industrial applications. The 340 used the C-135 IH-built gasoline or D-166 diesel four-cylinder engines as their power plants. The rear frame for the tractors incorporated a hydraulic filter element and used the transmission lubricant as the hydraulic oil, too, like 460–560 did.

The 340 employed a twelve-volt electrical system and a new engine, or optional transmission-driven hydraulic pump. The time-proved TA was not available on the 340. The I-340 had standard manual steering or optional hydraulic power steering. The F-340 was equipped with manual steering only. IH offered the 340 with optional Fast Hitch—available only on Farmall models—or industrial three-point hitch. The instrument panel was similar to the 460–560: large and flat in design. The I-340's drawbar power rating exceeded all

The International I-250 Utility prototype tractor as seen in 1956. The I-250 was a modified version of the I-350. This photo clearly shows the remote hydraulic valves that are now located at the base of the dash, not under the seat, as the 350 has. The shape of the new IH utility tractor line was slowly taking place. *State Historical Society of Wisconsin*

tractor was a nimble performer on the farm. While the I-240 was originally equipped with 17 inches of front-axle ground clearance, the F-240's axle was raised to 20 inches. I-240 tractor SN#528 was used in Nebraska Tractor Test #668. The power results recorded were nearly identical to the Farmall 240. The I-240 had a list price of $2,363.31, which, when compared to the lower horsepower John Deere that listed at $2,311.25, was a better purchase in terms of dollars per horsepower.

When IH introduced the 340 series tractor, it unveiled a totally new design. Using similar sheet-metal styling as the 460–560, along with a similar paint scheme, the 340 looked like a medium-sized tractor. Offered in both Farmall and Utility versions, the 340 utility

This photo, dated July 7, 1956, shows the new IH Farmall 400 tractor. From the length of the hood, it is evident that IH had already replaced its reliable four-cylinder engine with a longer six-cylinder version. Clearly, IH had started early in the development of a six-cylinder engine tractor program. In this prototype, IH had already placed the hydraulic valves at the base of the steering support. The special feature of this tractor is the unique underslung exhaust system. Forward operator visibility was never better. *State Historical Society of Wisconsin*

Shown here at the "New World of Profit" showing, this new Farmall tractor has the entire crowd's attention as the operator points out several features of using smooth six-cylinder power. Later, after the arena show, IH dealers would get a firsthand look at these new Farmalls. *State Historical Society of Wisconsin*

of the three-plow competitors in its class. IH built 7,210 Farmall versions from 1958 to 1963. The I-340 model produced 11,737 tractors.

One interesting variation of the I-340 was the I-340 Grove. Here, IH used an I-340 tractor equipped with special sheet-metal cowling and fenders for grove farming. The 340 Grove had the word "Grove" stamped below the "340"on the tractor's hood emblems for easy identification. Due to their specialized application, 340 Groves are quite rare today.

New Big Six-Cylinder Power: 460–560–660 Tractors

On a hot, sunny June 28, 1958, IH gave the town of Harvard, Illinois, the sneak peak of a lifetime. On that day,

local IH dealer Andy Anderson hauled a new Farmall tractor into town. After turning on Ayer Street (Harvard's main street), Anderson's truck pulled over and unloaded a tractor that made people look twice. This was a big tractor, unlike any Farmall that anyone had ever seen before. Andy hopped up on the tractor and made two circles around the downtown block before parking in front of Flores department store. The town was abuzz like bees in a hive. The news of this new Farmall spread to the countryside quickly, and farmers came to town and looked, and looked again, at the new big power tractor that was coming from IH. It was the 560 Farmall.

Farmers asked questions and IH reps answered, for example,

Q: "Is it really a five-plow tractor?"
A: "Yes."
Q: "What happened to the batteries? Where is the hydraulic pump?"
A: "Batteries are tucked under the hood and the hydraulic pump is internally mounted for a cleaner look."
Q: "Quite a bit longer than the Farmall 450?"
A: "No, the wheelbase and turning radius are the same. The new styling just makes it look longer."
Q: "Did you change the transmission much?"
A: "Just gear speed changes to match the new horsepower… We don't believe in changes that don't really improve the product. There are some other things in this tractor that have proved themselves in the past, and we know farmers will continue to demand them." (The last statement ended up being one IH would wish it had never said, when it became very obvious the 560 had some major flaws.)

The new easy-to-see instrument panel and easy-to-reach hydraulic controls were a big hit with those giving the 560 an "exam." The power steering was especially well received. After a few hours of show and tell, it was time for the 560 to return. Anderson loaded it onto the truck, and it was taken back to IH until its official showing on July 18, 1958.

A New World of Power

If you are the largest farm tractor manufacturer in the world, when you introduce a whole new series of machines, you do it in a big way. That is exactly what IH did in its "New World of Power" tractor introduction at the Harvester Testing Farm in Hinsdale, Illinois, in July of 1958. Here dealers saw IH's all-new lineup of really big tractors for the modern farmer. To say that the show itself was big could be considered an understatement. Each two-day show featured 65 acres of action-packed machinery displays and demos, and 80,000 square feet of tent space. The script for each show was 310 pages and weighed more than three pounds! The show employed 180 people, and had its

Nebraska Tractor Tests: 1958			
Model	**Fuel**	**Test No.**	**Belt HP**
Farmall 140	Gasoline	666	23.01
Farmall 240	Gasoline	667	30.82
Farmall 340	Gasoline	665	34.74

Roll 'em out! was heard as the new Farmall lineup left the show arena. Here an LPG-powered Farmall moves out for another group of tractors to be demonstrated in the arena. IH had more than 100 new tractors on display for dealers to see. *State Historical Society of Wisconsin*

own post office, barbershop, restaurant, and even bus line. A total of 12,000 IH dealers from the United States, Canada, and 25 foreign countries watched a seemingly endless parade of power: Seventy-six Farmalls along with 110 implements passed in front of them. Another 250 tractors and 260 implements were demonstrated or displayed. This was IH's BIG show.

The emphasis was on power—huge six-cylinder gasoline and diesel power. Leading the charge with more power was the new 62-horsepower tractor model called the 560. Its little brother had been the 52 horsepower model 460. There were also the midsize 36-horsepower model 340 and the 32-horsepower 240, both economical to operate and fuel economy leaders in their class. Rounding out the "New World of Power" was the 23-horsepower model 140 tractor, a newly restyled Cub, and Cub Lo-Boys.

During the "Parade of Power" in the main tent, IH choreographed a couple of new tractor introductions to music and dance. The Kilgore, Texas, College "Rangerettes" were hired by IH to be part of the show. The Rangerettes blended high-stepping, synchronized dancing with the action of new IH tractors. Using their familiar "suitcase" dance routine, the Rangerettes spelled out the words New World of Power in the opening act. While "dancing" with IH 340 Utility tractors mounted with Wagner front loaders, the Rangerettes drew a huge applause. Ironically, the 27-member troupe were the only women in the show.

The show would nearly have been a disaster had it not been for some good luck and timing. On the evening of July 14 a typical Midwestern thunderstorm rolled through the Hinsdale area, bringing high winds that blew over the 90x210-foot work tent. Nearly

a hundred new tractors were parked inside the tent when it blew down. Luckily, damage was mostly limited to the tractor mufflers, air stacks, and grilles. By 9 A.M. the next day, all but two tractors had been repaired and were ready for the big show.

After the show, many dealers returned home with renewed vigor for IH sales. Many were overheard making comments like, "I can only think how envious our competitors must feel now," or, "We came home with the renewed feeling that IH is first in farm equipment." Dealers were expected to sell more tractors to help expand IH's market share.

The 560 and 460 were offered in diesel-, gasoline-, and LPG-powered versions. The 560 diesel used an IH-built model D-282 six-cylinder engine of 282-ci displacement. The gasoline and LPG versions of the 560 used a C-263 six-cylinder engine that had a 263-ci displacement. The 460 diesel was powered by a D-236 IH six-cylinder engine, while the gasoline and LPG tractors used a C-221 six-cylinder engine. All the diesel engines used a glow plug starting system. IH had abandoned the old method of starting the engine on gasoline and then switching it over to diesel. This new design meant fewer parts and linkages, which led to a simple, cleaner-looking tractor. The gasoline engines still used the same IH updraft-style carburetors and Ensign LPG equipment that the previous 350–450 series had used.

The 560 was touted as the "World's most powerful row-crop tractor!" This was true for the time. Its big six-cylinder engine had the power to cultivate up to 100 acres per day using a six-row

cultivator. It could plow 30 acres a day when teamed with a five-bottom plow. It could do almost any job a farmer had faster and better than ever imagined. The silky smooth IH power steering was built into the tractor design from the start, and was not an add-on, as it was with the competitors. This was a major change for IH, as the steering rod no longer ran across the top of the engine. It was repositioned to run alongside the engine frame rail (similar to the position first used on the Farmall C). The super deluxe seat featured a backrest support, like the 450s had but with a smoother seat shock absorber and suspension spring.

The four-plow 460 was also touted by IH as a leader in power, performance,

efficiency, economy, comfort, convenience, strength, and style. Nothing else even came close to the 460! Big six-cylinder smoothness teamed up with traditional IH dependability. With the extra power of the 460, the operator could shift up and throttle back for maximum efficiency.

IH had its "New World of Power" tractor series tested at Nebraska, to prove they were, in fact, the new leaders. Farmall 560 tractor SN#502 was used in Tractor Test #671. Here the 560 proved that it had the right stuff by delivering more than 65 belt horsepower, making it the true king of its class in power. The Oliver 880 was its closest competition, with 64 belt horsepower. Farmall 460 diesel SN#720 set new

This new 63-horsepower International 660 standard tractor sure draws a crowd! It should, the new six-cylinder engine offered in gasoline, LPG, or diesel power, makes this the right tractor for any standard tread application. Direct starting diesel engines are easy to start and easy on fuel too. Optional power steering makes long days seem less tiring. *State Historical Society of Wisconsin*

This photo of the display yard at the Hinsdale Show clearly shows the excited crowds that were generated at the show. Dealers from across the United States, Canada, and foreign countries swarmed over the new power of IH tractors. The switch from four-cylinder engines to big six-cylinder power plants was the logical choice for more tractor power that customers demanded. *State Historical Society of Wisconsin*

records for tractor drawbar horsepower in its class. Farmall 340 SN#850 and Farmall 240 SN#505 also proved through testing that they were the new leaders for power and economy in their tractor classes too.

One of the selling points of the new 460–560 series was its operator convenience. In this case, IH really improved the tractor over previous models. The hydraulic touch control system had a change that made its operation much easier. Below the instrument panel were two or three (depending on options) hand-operated turn levers. These had decals by them that said "D-S." This stood for double (D) or single (S) action hydraulics. Now the operator could select which method of hydraulic valve operation he or she needed. By turning the lever to D, the operator could use double-action cylinders. Moving the

lever to S allowed single-acting cylinders to operate. It was very simple and no tools were needed, unlike that for the previous series.

The 460 and 560 each offered IH's time-proven mechanical TA as an available option. Another transmission option was the high-speed low and reverse gears on the 560s. On 560s equipped with this option, first gear had a 40 percent increase in speed, while reverse had a 60 percent increase in speed. This proved a handy option for loader or shuttle operation work.

Another transmission option was the "Fast Reverser" on the 460 tractors. This option provided the operator with selective full reverse, operating at about 22 percent faster than the forward gear. To operate the "Fast Reverser," you would choose the gear in which you plan to operate (IH recommends third

gear for loader work) and when approaching the loading material, depress the clutch and move the Reverser lever all the way forward. Release clutch, load bucket. To move backward, depress clutch, and move the Reverser lever all the way rearward. Release the clutch slowly. This was an attempt to build a shuttle shifting–style transmission. Tractor competitor Ford offered a partial shuttle shift using its "Selecto-Speed" transmission. Here the operator moved a cowl-mounted lever to pick both the gear speed and direction he or she needed. This worked fine if the transmission was adjusted right, but the design of the "Selecto-Speed" transmission used bands that needed frequent adjustment.

Both the 460 and 560 could be equipped with IH's famous Fast Hitch. Traction control was an available option, too, just as it was on the 350–450s.

This orange-painted I-460 is equipped with a pull-type rotary mower that makes quick work of a roadside near Green Bay, Wisconsin. IH offered specially painted orange tractors to local, state, and federal highway departments. The "Highway Orange" painted tractors had a higher visibility to motorists than red-painted ones. *State Historical Society of Wisconsin*

IH built several specialized versions of the I-460. One version was the 460 Wheat Land, used for farming in wheat-growing areas. The 460 Wheat Land had new front and rear platforms, a "Wheat Land" model symbol plate, and new fenders that used the crown of the I-560 tractor fenders. A choice of hand- or foot-operated clutch and TA was also offered. Another version was the 460 Hi-Utility. This was similar to the regular 460 Utility, except that it had an increased ground clearance of 4.3 inches from the use of Farmall 460 rear axles, wheels, and tires, and modified front-axle extensions and steering knuckle assemblies. The speeds

This I-240 Utility is teamed with a two-row Fast Hitch–mounted planter. The low profile of the I-240 gave the operator outstanding visibility, front or rear. The optional power-adjusted rear wheels made changing rear wheel tread a snap, not a chore. This 240 had front wheel weights to maintain steering control with the rear-mounted planter. *State Historical Society of Wisconsin*

passed in front of them. Another 250 tractors and 260 implements were demonstrated or displayed. This was IH's BIG show.

The emphasis was on power—huge six-cylinder gasoline and diesel power. Leading the charge with more power was the new 62-horsepower tractor model called the 560. Its little brother had been the 52 horsepower model 460. There were also the midsize 36-horsepower model 340 and the 32-horsepower 240, both economical to operate and fuel economy leaders in their class. Rounding out the "New World of Power" was the 23-horse-power model 140 tractor, a newly restyled Cub, and Cub Lo-Boys.

During the "Parade of Power" in the main tent, IH choreographed a couple of new tractor introductions to music and dance. The Kilgore, Texas, College "Rangerettes" were hired by IH to be part of the show. The Rangerettes blended high-stepping, synchronized dancing with the action of new IH tractors. Using their familiar "suitcase" dance routine, the Rangerettes spelled out the words New World of Power in the opening act. While "dancing" with IH 340 Utility tractors mounted with Wagner front loaders, the Rangerettes drew a huge applause. Ironically, the 27-member troupe were the only women in the show.

The show would nearly have been a disaster had it not been for some good luck and timing. On the evening of July 14 a typical Midwestern thunderstorm rolled through the Hinsdale area, bringing high winds that blew over the 90x210-foot work tent. Nearly a hundred new tractors were parked inside the tent when it blew down. Luckily, damage was mostly limited to the tractor mufflers, air stacks, and grilles. By 9 A.M. the next day, all but two tractors had been repaired and were ready for the big show.

After the show, many dealers returned home with renewed vigor for IH sales. Many were overheard making comments like, "I can only think how envious our competitors must feel now," or, "We came home with the re-

Powering the IH bale elevator is the rare white grille version of the 504 Utility tractor. The 45-horsepower models 504 and its little brother 404 were the first IH tractors equipped with an integral draft control three-point rear hitch. *State Historical Society of Wisconsin*

newed feeling that IH is first in farm equipment." Dealers were expected to sell more tractors to help expand IH's market share.

The 560 and 460 were offered in diesel-, gasoline-, and LPG-powered versions. The 560 diesel used an IH-built model D-282 six-cylinder engine of 282-ci displacement. The gasoline and LPG versions of the 560 used a C-263 six-cylinder engine that had a 263-ci displacement. The 460 diesel was powered by a D-236 IH six-cylinder engine, while the gasoline and LPG tractors used a C-221 six-cylinder engine. All the diesel engines used a glow plug starting system. IH had abandoned the old method of starting the engine on gaso-

Nebraska Tractor Tests: 1958			
Model	**Fuel**	**Test No.**	**Belt HP**
Farmall 560	Diesel	669	59.48
Farmall 460	Gasoline	670	49.47
Farmall 560	Gasoline	671	63.03
Farmall 460	Diesel	672	50.10
I-460 Utility	Diesel	673	50.01
I-460 Utility	Gasoline	674	49.79
Farmall 560	LPG	675	60.11
Farmall 460	LPG	676	49.85

This rare shot of the International 460 Grove shows the massive cowling used to protect the operator from tree limbs and other hazards. The low-mounted front headlights are located under the grille, out of harm's way. The orange trees in the background are the typical crop of choice for grove tractor operation. Very few 460 Groves were ever built; only a handful are known to exist today. *State Historical Society of Wisconsin*

of a horizontal air filter element above the rear hood. IH did not build 560 Diesels with turbos from the factory. The turbocharger kit sold for $462 in 1967.

IH Introduces the 660 Standard

In Tractor Change Notice #508, dated May 1958, IH released a new 61-horsepower-model, standard-tread-only tractor called the 660. The 660 was similar to the 560 in that it used both the C-263 gasoline and D-282 diesel six-cylinder engines. But the C-263 used a different carburetor and distributor and was modified from the 560 version to operate at 2,400 rpm. A new torsion vibration damper was added, as were new valves, a fan pulley, and a governor spring.

A 12-inch single-plate dry disc foot-operated clutch also controlled the TA. If a hand-operated clutch were ordered, this lever would control both the main drive clutch and TA.

The 660 was styled the same as the 560 except that a cast spacer having the same front design as the top grille was added below the lower grille. This made the tractor look larger. IH used full floating stub axles, which were splined to the wheel hubs. Any wheel tread adjustments were made by the position of the rim on the wheel. Planetary-type final drives used their own lubricant, separate from the rest of the transmission. Heavy cast-iron wheels were used with 18–26 tires.

The 660 front axle used a solid 5-inch-diameter bar that had a fixed

tread with a solid stay rod and cast front wheels. A wide front axle was available only on the 660. Hydraulic power steering was also available as an attachment.

On 10-13-58, IH released the production of an LP gas–powered 660. This, too, was similar to the 560, except for the fuel tank support angle assemblies, exhaust pipe heat shield, engine, governor control rod, filter to the regulator fuel line, and exhaust pipe. To help identify the LP gas models from other tractors, the letter L was stamped on the serial number plate, and the words LP Gas were printed on the tractor nameplate on each side of the hood.

The I-660 diesel carried a list price of $5,710.81 compared to the I-560's list price of $4,844.41. Both were comparably priced to the John Deere 730 Standard ($4,808.90) and the 830 ($5,794.90). The 67-horsepower Case 900B had a list price of $6,042, making the I-660 diesel with 78 PTO appear very low priced.

The "Other" Farmall 360 and 460

An interesting note to the 460–560 tractors is that originally IH was going to label these as the 360 and 460. This would follow the numbering system IH had used in the previous 300–350 and 400–450 tractors. Both the 360 and 460 were released for production by IH in Tractor Change Letters #84 and #85, dated 1-30-57. The model 360 tractor had the following features:

- A twelve-volt electrical system.
- New fenders with wider tire coverage.
- A new C-221 six-cylinder gasoline-powered engine, or new D-236 diesel-powered engine.
- A new air cleaner intake located under the hood and in front of

Nebraska Tractor Tests: 1959			
Model	**Fuel**	**Test No.**	**PTO Power**
I-660	Diesel	715	78.78
I-660	Gasoline	721	81.39
I-660	LPG	722	80.63

the radiator (although this never actually occurred until the 06 series was released in 1963).

- Newly designed clutch housing and rear frame, incorporating a lubricant filter, and also using the rear frame as the hydraulic reservoir. The lubricant in the rear frame was compatible with both the IH Touch Control Fluid and IH Torque Amplifier Transmission Additive fluids.
- A new hood and radiator grille, featuring horizontal crossbars at the lower section, and a new perforated contour upper section. The hood matched the contour, with the lower panels being separate pieces. This new hood and grille used a two-tone color combination.

The 460 was identical in new features to the 360, with the exception of the engines. The 460 used a C-263 six-cylinder gasoline engine and a D-282 six-cylinder diesel engine.

Both the 360 and 460 were to be offered in the following versions: Farmall row-crop, Hi-Clearance, Diesel, Diesel Hi-Clearance, Utility, and Diesel Utility. Ironically, in Tractor Change Letter #84-A, dated September 11,1957, IH had a last-minute change of mind and decided to label the old 360 model as the "new" 460, and the "old" 460 became the 560. Sound confusing? Yes.

IH's highly successful urban product called the Cub Cadet was actually built using the transmission and differential found in the Cub and Cub Lo-Boy. Here at the Louisville IH plant, where both lines were made, an engineer points out the similar parts. The bold steps IH took in developing the Cub Cadet tractor paid off many times over. *State Historical Society of Wisconsin*

Chapter 2
The 1960s
SIX-CYLINDER HORSEPOWER
DOMINATES THE MARKETPLACE

The dramatic change in farming in the 1960s was unlike nearly any other time in history. The switch from 40–70 horsepower tractors to 60–120 horsepower tractors and the implements to match them was unmatched this century. Many aftermarket or "will fitter" or the local engine shops were altering tractors to make more horsepower—even if the tractor couldn't absorb the extra power very long.

The sport of organized tractor-pulling contests exploded rapidly. These were typically held during the county fair or local town festival. Farmers would boast that their tractor was best, but on the track they had to prove it. Some cheated (anything was legal until you were caught); some still do cheat at these events today. IH and the other tractor manufacturers of this decade paid very close attention to what was happening in tractor pulls. Sometimes the events were a way to do some real R&D testing of ideas that were on the wild side. The main point that tractor companies learned was that as the farms became larger, the need for more mechanized, efficient, bigger, faster, and stronger equipment would soon be here. IH took one of the first steps.

Big Horsepower Ahead of Its Time: IH 4300 Four-Wheel-Drive Tractor

IH unveiled its first "behemoth" of a tractor in the model 4300 four-wheel drive. The Hough Industrial Division of IH in Libertyville, Illinois, built the series. Big, raw power was the 4300's calling card. Using an IH-built six-cylinder turbocharged diesel engine with a displacement of 817 ci, the 4300 had more than 180 drawbar horsepower. It was a huge tractor for its day, and it was way ahead of its time. A PTO was not offered on the 4300. This beast of a four-wheel-drive tractor weighed in at over 29,800 pounds—almost 15 tons!—and needed air brakes to stop it.

The 4300 featured articulated power steering, eight-speed selective range transmission, and outboard planetary final reduction axles as standard equipment. An all-weather operator cab was optional. Air conditioning was not offered. A massive, hydraulically operated drawbar at the rear of the tractor allowed the attachment of large earth scrapers and other implements. Only 45 4300 IH four-wheel drives were built during the 1960–1963 production life

Farmall version of the model 404 pulling a moldboard plow. Notice the extra weights on the front wheels and frame to give stability in transport and aid in turning. Tractors using heavy rear-mounted implements needed this extra ballast at the front of the tractor. *Author Collection*

IH's entry into the four-wheel-drive market came with its model 4300 tractor. Powered by a six-cylinder, turbocharged, 817-ci diesel engine, the 4300 produced more than 203 drawbar horsepower. This was too large for some farms, and most of the 45 tractors that IH built from 1961 through 1965 were sold to industrial users. The 4300 had air brakes and a rear hydraulic lifting drawbar and was available with an optional operator's cab. A fully mounted 10-bottom moldboard plow was specially made for the 4300 at IH's Stockton (California) Works. *Author Collection*

of the model, nearly all of them custom built for their owners. While IH definitely didn't set any sales records with the 4300, it did put a big ripple in the tractor horsepower pond.

The implements to match the 4300 were big too. Field cultivators 45 or even 60 feet wide were used behind them. Tandem earth scrapers were also used. IH even built one (and possibly two) fully mounted 10-bottom moldboard plow for the 4300. It easily handled this implement.

Paying the Price: Transmission Recall of the 60 series

In 1958, IH was just starting to sell a lot of the new 460 and 560 tractors. But a growing number of reports from

the field started first trickling in, then streaming in, to IH, describing final drive failures on the 460 and 560. IH was getting very nervous about these reports. In many cases, final drive failure was occurring in the first 50 to 100 hours of operation. Something needed to be done—immediately. IH engineers worked feverishly to find a fix. Every day that passed another hundred (or so it seemed) tractors were failing. Farmers and dealers were very, very upset with IH. No one knew the answer to the problem, and no one could remedy it. Weeks and months went by, and more final drives continued to fail.

IH engineers finally identified part of the problem as the design of the bull gears and the bull pinion and brake

shaft. In Tractor Change Letter #19730, dated January 23, 1959, IH engineering revised the bull gears and bull pinion and brake shaft to a 125-micro-inch finish and modified the curve of the gear teeth. This was done to improve load-carrying ability and (hopefully) overcome customer complaints. But it was not the answer to IH's problem.

In March 1959, IH modified the bull gear hub assembly. This did not help much, either. In Tractor Change Letter #20309, dated April 1959, IH revised the differential bevel gears by removing the oil holes and replacing them with oil grooves on the back face of the gear. This was done to ensure lubrication to the outer face of the gear. Finally IH did some "cutting and chopping" on the differential gears by adding a chamfer on the sides of the tooth profile at the OD of the gear. This was supposed to increase the thrust area of the gear and eliminate sharp cutting edges to reduce wear. These changes, too, did not solve the final drive problem.

By this time, hundreds of IH dealers and their customers were becoming highly impatient with the very slow progress Tractor Engineering seemed to be making on the final drive problems. Dealers were having 560s returned to them, and some owners never came back to get them. A few owners filed legal action against IH, accusing the company of selling "lemon" tractors. Many longtime loyal IH customers were pushed away by IH's apparent lack of care and action. A number of them went to Deere and never looked back. IH knew that the final drive in 460–560s had been "maxed out" before prototypes were even made. (This fact was discovered during field testing of the Super MTA.) Why had the company ignored its findings? Was IH so big that it believed anything it made was the greatest ever? Competitor John Deere would later capitalize on this arrogance and twist it for its own unique style of marketing. Deere still practices this today. It is the master of "remarketing." It convinces its customers that anything it makes is not only the best, but is also a totally new idea that only John Deere could invent!

In June of 1959, IH pushed the panic button. In Tractor Change Letter #20624, IH listed a nearly completely revised rear axle and differential unit for the 460, 560, and 660. The new parts provided for the use of a heavier differential case, tapered bearings, bull pinion, and brake shaft cage and bearing. These changes were to be implemented along with the previously announced modifications to solve the problem. IH was gutting the rear end for a total overhaul.

The company launched a field modification campaign. Dealers would be given the tools, parts, and know-how to fix the affected 460s and 560s. For those dealers who did not own the

This 1961 photo shows an IH dealer pointing out the hydraulic features of the Farmall 560 Brass Tacks demonstrator. IH had special demonstrator decal packages made that were either factory or dealer installed. The tractor was then to be used for on-farm demonstrations and later retailed. *Author Collection*

shop facilities to handle this influx of repairs, IH set up district and regional "tent cities" where the affected tractors would be reconditioned by IH personnel. At these tent cities, teams of IH-trained technicians would update the tractors (both new and used) to the improved design. It was not uncommon to see well over 100 tractors parked at these repair sites, either awaiting repair or newly repaired.

Nearly all of IH's competitors had a field day with the tent-city idea. They made claims of how IH was scrapping hundreds of tractors and offering cash to buy back problematic units from their owners—neither of which was entirely true. In the rush to have "big power" first, IH had given itself a big black eye instead. This was due to rushing the engineering process and not fully testing an area IH knew could be the weak link.

In the aftermath of this program, IH announced the availability of a "new" differential, bull pinion and bull gear as conversion packages for prior model tractors. The models affected were: Farmall Super MTA, 300, 350, 400, 450, and Super W6TA along with the International 300, 350, 400, and 450 tractors. These packages were the same ones being used in the 460–560 "re-work" program. It is doubtful whether many (if any) of these packages were sold, due to the fact that the tractors listed had much less engine horsepower, and failures in these models were not widespread.

All of the new 460 and 560 tractors in dealer stock didn't necessarily get the "full package" of field modification. Lowell Kittleson, former IH service representative, vividly remembers the 460–560 tractor recall program. He said, "All that happened was that the inner

This photo shows the rare white grille version of the Farmall 504 tractor pulling a four-bottom IH model 60 moldboard plow. The early 504 tractors shown in their advertising literature all had white-painted grille shells and sometimes white-painted wheel rims. The 504 was available in either row-crop (Farmall) or utility (International) versions. *State Historical Society of Wisconsin*

axle bearing was removed and reinstalled [in the place] where the outer axle bearing was. (The outer bearing was scrapped.) A new tapered roller bearing was installed in the inside of the axle and the repair was done." Sounded like a pretty simple fix. Just play "musical chairs" with the bearings. After a 460 or 560 had had the field update installed, a triangle was to be punched on the tractor serial number tag to signify that it had been updated.

With the tractor final drive problems IH was having, the production of Farmall 560 tractors slowed to a crawl in 1960, with only 6,510 tractors being made that year. Compared to that, IH had built 22,273 model 560s in 1959. The 460 Farmall production slowed to only 5,716 tractors built in 1960 versus 12,136 tractors in 1959. IH never regained its production momentum. In 1961, 1962, and 1963, IH averaged around 3,000 Farmall 460s per year and 10,000 Farmall 560s

per year. IH's competitors (mainly John Deere) were there to gain some tractor sales at IH's expense.

Selling Lemonade after Lemons...the 560 Demonstrators

As early as 1958, IH had a tractor demonstration program in place for the entire "New World of Power" tractor lineup. Once again this program was called the "Brass Tacks" tractor demo program. One change IH did make was

This Farmall 140 is pulling a Fast Hitch–mounted tandem disk harrow. The hydraulic lifting linkage is clearly shown in this photo. IH built more than 66,000 model 140s during its 1958 to 1979 production span. Only the Cub tractor had a longer production run (1947 to 1979). *Author Collection*

the elimination of a large wooden sign on the tractor's hood. Instead, decals were simply placed on the tractor to point out its features. All of the tractor models IH was making at the time could have been ordered from the factory with the demo decal set installed. These included the 660, 560, 460, 340, 240, 140, Cub, and Cub Lo-Boy. Eleven different decals pointed out the various features of the tractor. Not every tractor used every decal, though. Only the 660 could have all 11. The slogans on the decals were:

1. Operator Comfort
2. Operator Convenience
3. Conveniently Grouped Controls
4. Job Matched Speeds
5. Tailored Hydraulics
6. Completely Independent Power Take-Off
7. Time-Proved TA Power
8. Shimmy Proof Power Steering
9. Smooth Multi-Range Power
10. More Work at Lower Cost
11. Full Range Six Plow Power

As in the previous Brass Tacks demo program, IH did allow the use of dealer stock tractors to become demo models. This was, of course, providing the tractor met the equipment option criteria.

One aspect of this Brass Tacks demo program was that it was in effect in 1958, 1959, and 1960. The first demo program appears to have run from mid-1958 to the end of 1958. When the final drive "recall" was in effect, IH dropped the demo program. After the recall program was finished, IH revived the Brass Tacks demo program for one more run. This second-chance demo program ran from November 2, 1959, through October 31, 1960. This second wave of demos seemed to be the most remembered. This author believes IH revived the demo program not only to increase sales and regain the market share it had lost, but also as a goodwill gesture to show that even after a major product recall, IH still stood behind its tractors. It was hoped that this would restore the farmers' confidence in IH. For some it did, others had already jumped ship to Brand X.

IH realized the weakness in its tractor design in the early 1950s. Now IH had a tractor series ready to go head to head with the Deere "New Generation" series. These new tractors were the 706 and 806. Their future replacements would become part of a pattern of repeat "cookie cutter" engineering, just as the 560–460s had. Ultimately, the company itself that could not or would not

IH dealers had tractors for every size operation, whether it be the 63-horsepower model 656, the 7-horsepower Cub Cadet Original, or an IH 806 pedal tractor. Your IH dealer is the place to find the latest in IH parts, service, advice, and IH toys! Here, an IH salesperson is pointing out the easy-starting engine on this 656. *Author Collection*

The 404 was rated at 36 horsepower and offered as a gasoline or LPG power model only. It used an IH-built C-135 four-cylinder engine, and was governed at 2,000 rpm. IH built the 404 in both Farmall and utility-style versions.

The 504 was offered in gasoline, LPG, and Diesel power choices. All three were tested at Nebraska with the gas and LPG recording 46 horsepower while the diesel tested 45 horsepower. The gas and LPG engines were of a four-cylinder inline design with a displacement of 152 ci. The diesel engine had a 187-ci displacement. All three engines in the 504 were governed at 2,200 rpm.

In 1961, IH introduced the new model 606 Utility tractor. The 606 was not made in the Farmall version at all. Using a C-221 gasoline or LPG engine or a D-236 six-cylinder diesel engine, the 606 recorded 54 horsepower at its Nebraska Tractor test. The 606 offered as standard equipment hydrostatic steering, three-point rear hitch with draft control, and hydraulic oil cooler. A TA was offered as optional equipment to give the operator a total of 10 forward and 2 reverse speeds. The 606 was a real powerhouse in a smaller-sized tractor. During its production run from 1961 to 1967, IH built 7,438 units.

New Power and Operating Ease: 706 and 806 Tractors

Even before the peak of the 460–560 drive-train crisis in 1959, IH engineers knew that the handwriting was on the wall as to the longevity of the old "M"-style final drive. The M-style design had been the basic style of farm tractor used by IH for over the last 20 years. IH needed something new, an entirely clean-sheet-design tractor that could face the increasingly massive horsepower challenges of today and tomorrow, a tractor capable of handling 90 horsepower or more. And with the 1960 introduction of the "New Generation" tractors by competitor John Deere, IH needed a new tractor now more than ever.

In the summer of 1963, IH announced its answer to Deere's "New Generation." Three models constituted

produce a power-shift transmission tractor in the 1970s would fail.

Technology Advances in Tractor Design

IH introduced two new tractor models in 1960, the 404 and 504. Both featured many advancements in engineering that the rest of the industry would copy. The major advance was the use of a dry, replaceable, cartridge-type engine air filter. The three-point hitch with draft control soon became standard on the next generation of IH tractors. A torsion bar connected internally

to the tractor's top link arm would sense the draft load. Another major design was the use of a totally hydrostatic power steering system. With this, there was no mechanical connection to be turned between the steering wheel and the wheels. The increased working loads being generated in the hydraulic and transmission systems closely matched the increase in engine horsepower. IH devised adding a hydraulic oil cooler. This radiator-type device was mounted in front if the tractor's radiator. The 504 had the new air filter, oil cooler, and the hydrostatic steering.

Nebraska Tractor Tests: 1962

Model	Fuel	Test No.	PTO Power
Farmall 404	Gasoline	818	36.70
Farmall 504	Gasoline	819	46.20
Farmall 504	LPG	820	44.36
Farmall 504	Diesel	816	45.99

this new series of tractors, labeled the 06 series. The first was the 54-horsepower model 606 Utility tractor (which was generically an I-460 Utility with power steering), which was released in 1961 and remained in production through 1967. The 606 used either a six-cylinder C-221 gasoline or D-226 diesel engine. The other two were the 73 PTO horsepower model 706 and the big 94 PTO horsepower model 806.

The 606 used either a six-cylinder C-221 gasoline or D-226 diesel engine, and had such features as TA, power steering, rear fast-hitch, and cushioned operator seat. The 606 series had 7,438 tractors built. The real stars of the 06 series, however, were the new 706 and 806. These were the tractors IH needed to regain market-share leadership.

The 706 and 806 were both offered in standard tread (International) and row-crop (Farmall) configurations. The 706 and 806 featured an all-new transmission with a hydraulically controlled TA, new hydraulic system, and fully hydrostatic power steering. The use of self-adjusting hydraulic power brakes was a first for IH. This greatly reduced the pressure the operator needed to apply to the pedal to stop these huge tractors. An independent PTO unit was an available option that gave the owner the choice of either a single 1,000-rpm PTO unit or a dual shaft 540–1,000-rpm PTO.

Powering the 706 was either the C-263 or C-291 six-cylinder gasoline- or LPG-fueled engine. The 706 diesel used a D-282 six-cylinder glow plug start diesel engine until it was replaced by the direct start six-cylinder model D310 German diesel. Farmall 706 SN#37237, built November 1, 1966, was equipped with the first D-310 engine. The 706 tractor recorded a 73 PTO horsepower rating at the Nebraska Tractor Test.

The 806 used a C-301 six-cylinder "sleeveless" engine as the power plant for the gasoline- and LPG-powered tractors. This engine was basically a C-263 engine like that used in the 560 but with a very interesting twist. The valve covers on the 806 gas and LPG tractors are made of cast iron, the 706 has a stamped steel cover. Why? When IH engineers fitted the C-301 into the 806 chassis, there was a large gap between the valve cover and the side hood panel line when viewed from the side. Farmers would surely question this, as the 806 diesel did not have this gap. (The D-361 diesel engine was taller.) To correct this impression, an optical illusion was created by nearly doubling the valve cover height. This taller valve cover filled the gap and kept farmers from asking why such a small engine was in a large tractor.

The 806 diesel used the new D-361 six-cylinder dry sleeve direct start diesel engine. Initially the 806 used IH's own RD-style fuel injection pump. This was later switched for performance and serviceability to the "Rosa Master"-style pump when the 1206 was introduced. The D-361 quickly became a legend in its own time. Power, torque, and long, long life were all characteristics of the D-361. Even today, it is not unusual to find 806 diesel tractors that have logged in excess of 20,000 hours of operation still running strong, and they have "never been touched," meaning never overhauled. The secret to the D-361's longevity eludes this author to this day. It does seem clear that when IH switched the D-361 into the D and DT-407, engine life was decreased for some unknown reason.

To help start the D-361 in cooler weather, an optional ether starting assist

Billed as "The world's most powerful tricycle tractor," the all-new Farmall 806 gave new life to IH's tractor sales. Available in gasoline, LPG, or diesel engine power, the 806 had a fleet of optional equipment to fit any farm. IH made more than 50,000 806 tractors during its 1963 to 1967 production run. At the time of this writing, the author currently owns Farmall 806 SN #501 (the first 806 built). *State Historical Society of Wisconsin*

aid was offered. This was mounted on the left side of the tractor in front of the battery. Pulling a cable when the tractor was being started injected ether into the intake manifold, allowing the engine to start easier in cold weather. While the cable-operated ether start generally worked fine, in very cold conditions the cable could freeze or stick, causing the engine to possibly overload on ether and resulting in serious damage. To overcome these problems, IH switched to an electrically operated solenoid ether start. The new electric kit used a push-button switch mounted on the instrument panel and a new combination solenoid/ether can holder. This new kit was offered on F-806 SN#30122, I-806 SN#6658, F-1206 SN#10235, and I-1206 SN#8040 and above.

The first 806 diesels were equipped with IH's own fuel injection pump, commonly called the "RD" pump. Shortly after the 1206 series was released, the 806 diesels had the "RD" pump replaced by the new Rosa Master-style injection pump. The model DBGFC 637-3DH-injection pump with speed advance and fuel return bypass was used. One easy way to spot an RD-style engine is to look for a separate cast-iron oil filler elbow on the right side of the engine. On tractors equipped with the RD pump, the oil dipstick was separate from the oil fill. The Rosa Master pump engines used a common oil tube for filling the engine and holding the dipstick. After the 1206 introduction, IH did offer a conversion kit to replace the RD pump with the Rosa Master, if the farmer desired. This kit was announced in January of 1966. IH even built a very limited run of 200 model 706 tractors with the RD pump. These tractors are very rare today.

A new operator platform and control layout were but a few of the newer features the 06 series had. The operator now sat on a cushioned, upholstered seat with dual spring suspension and wraparound back cushion design. The seat was located ahead of the tractor's rear axle, giving the operator a smoother ride and better forward view. You could adjust for seat height and

The little brother to the 806 was the 706 Farmall. Rated at 73 PTO horsepower, the 706 was very popular in sales, with more than 52,000 tractors built. The 706 and 806 were IH's first tractors to use a hydraulically actuated TA transmission attachment. This new TA gave positive engine braking power to the tractor. *State Historical Society of Wisconsin*

operator's weight, or raise the seat for driving the tractor while standing. On November 1, 1964, a new Deluxe Seat assembly was released for production on the 706–806 and 504 tractors. This new Deluxe Seat assembly offered a two-piece backrest cushion for increased operator comfort. Tractors above the serial numbers listed below could have the new Deluxe Seat assembly: F-504 SN#10287, F-706 SN#19250, I-706 SN#3000, F-806 SN#14500, and I-806 SN#3400.

The transmission shifting controls were now located on the right-hand side of the steering tower. The inside lever controls the range and direction of the tractor. Two ranges (high and low), along with a neutral and reverse, were all controlled by moving this lever in a straight line. A second lever directly beside the range lever controlled the tractor's speed gear selection. Here the operator had a choice of four speeds.

These four gears could be used in any range, even reverse. If the optional TA was added, a total of 16 forward and 8 reverse speeds could be used.

IH had only one major problem area with shifting on 706 and 806. This was the Hi-Low shifting fork and shaft. Service Bulletin #S-1493, dated November 16, 1965, states this change. The change IH made was to reduce the bolt hole size on the fork to 5/16 inches from the previous 3/8-inch size, because breakage was commonly reported there. The tapped hole in the fork shaft was thus changed accordingly. When the "old style" shaft or fork broke, both had to be updated.

Directly below the two shifting levers was the park lock pedal. This was used by the operator to put the tractor into a positive engaged park position, so he wouldn't have to rely on the brakes or the dangerous practice of putting the tractor in gear to hold the machine. IH

A single-front-wheel, gasoline-powered Farmall 706 has a two-row wide-mounted #30 IH cotton stripper attached. IH was the innovator in mechanized cotton harvesting, building the first successful self-propelled cotton harvester. IH continued to use tractors as the cotton harvester's base unit until specialized harvesting chassis were built in the late 1960s. *State Historical Society of Wisconsin*

had a problem with the park lock pedal design. It seemed that as the operator would reach to grab the shift levers, his foot would typically extend and step on the pedal. This would cause the park lock pawl to engage, and serious transmission tooth damage would occur. To correct this, IH had a "mandatory" field changeover program to convert the foot-operated park lock tractors to a newly designed hand lever-operated style. By using a hand-operated lever, IH found that the park lock pawl could not be accidentally activated. Another weak link in the park lock design was the use of a 3/8-inch threaded turnbuckle linkage, which was prone to breakage and bending. To solve this, IH switched to a linkage made from 7/16-inch stock. All

of the 1206 tractors have the 7/16-inch rod linkage, while F-706 SN#27484, I-706 SN#4415, F-806 SN#21639, I-806 SN#5238, and above all have the larger rod linkage.

The hydraulically powered TA had its control lever on the left-hand side of the steering tower. This totally TA design used the tractor's pressurized hydraulic oil to engage and disengage the unit. A hydraulic pump was internally mounted to a valve assembly for this purpose. This valve was called the MCV, or Multiple Control Valve. It not only controlled the TA's operation, but also supplied hydraulic oil for the power steering and brake circuits too. The MCV pump was driven from the IPTO drive gear in the speed transmission

housing. This IPTO drive gear was coupled directly to the main clutch pressure plate. This shaft had live power whenever the engine was running, which was needed for the operation of the steering and brakes much more than the TA. If the spline on the shaft rounded over, or the engine stopped, halting the pump, the operator would still have manual brakes and steering for vehicle control.

As the tractor's hydraulics were being called upon to do more tasks, the need for cleaner and cooler hydraulic oil became even greater. To get cleaner hydraulic oil, IH used a large cylindrical-shaped, throwaway-style paper hydraulic filter. This filter was easy to change by simply removing a cover. Keeping the hydraulic oil cool, however, was another problem. With the filter, IH used an externally mounted oil cooler bolted ahead of the engine radiator. This was fine until the radiator needed cleaning, then the cooler had to be unbolted and then reattached after cleaning. To solve this, IH designed a new "swing-out" style of oil cooler. This allowed the cooler to be moved out of the way for better cleaning simply by removing two wing nuts. IH added this change fairly early in the 06 series production, with the new style "swing-out" coolers first appearing on F-706 SN#15186, I-706 SN#2350, F-806 SN#12052, and I-806 SN#2783.

Even with all of these new features and transmission speeds, the operator still needed to know how fast he was going. IH could have used the multi-colored band tachometer/speedometer that not only read engine speed but also miles per hour in each gear. This was what the 450 through 660 had used. Instead, IH used a tachometer that was plain black with white print engine speed only; a speed chart decal on the panel covered the regulator. Many customers complained to IH that they greatly disliked this new tachometer and wanted the old style color tachometer/speedometer back. Consequently, IH changed to a colored combination speedometer/tachometer in late 1964. The F-706 SN#19250,

"Ship 'em out the door!" was the cry heard at the Farmall Works in Rock Island, Illinois. In this undated photo, a Farmall 806 diesel (1963 or 1964 model) awaits to be released from its assembly stand for final dynamometer testing. IH was building 706, 806, 1206, 504, and 656 tractors all on one common assembly line at Farmall. Notice the rear wheels are reversed for narrow transport width. *Author Collection*

I-706 SN#3000, F-806 SN#14500, I-806 SN#2529, and above all came equipped with the new speedometer/ tachometer assembly. Today finding an original "black face" tachometer can be very difficult.

The control levers for the remote hydraulic valves were located beside the operator's seat. Up to two valves could be ordered, and each valve could have outlets in both the rear of the tractor and the midsection, below the steering tower. Initially, short cast-iron levers were offered. However, Service Bulletin #S-1357, dated January 22, 1965, announced the switch to longer, tubular handles. This brought the levers closer to the operator and eliminated possible interference when the 706–806 tractors were used with 2MH or 2MHD corn pickers. IH continued to use these longer levers until 1976. The newly engineered remote hydraulic valves remained in IH's tractor program (in slightly modified form) until 1985.

They were easier to repair than the previous valve design and had an adjustable coupler-latching pressure feature. The hydraulically operated Fast Hitch or three-point rear hitch control lever, along with the hitch draft control lever, was also on the right side of the seat.

The 06 series heralded IH's announcement of its new style of self-sealing hydraulic couplings. These couplers were called the "Gold" couplers, and they replaced the previous "Silver"-style

Farmers were demanding a tractor with more power. IH had the answer with the industry's first 100+ PTO horsepower turbocharged diesel row-crop tractor. In this photo, dated June 17, 1964, the prototype International 1206 is shown. Notice the all-red-painted grille shell, wheels, and rear fenders. IH even had the word Turbo stamped below the 1206 model number on the side plate. *Author Collection*

couplers. The new Gold couplers featured a specifically designed poppet valve in the male half of the coupler. This allowed coupling to the female half—easy to do if there was pressure trapped in the line. You no longer needed to release the pressure in the line before coupling. Once the two halves were coupled together, the poppet valve would open and remain open. IH was very adamant in stating that the Gold couplers should be used as a pair. If Silver male couplings were used with Gold female couplings on heavy implements, a "lock-up" (failure to lower) would occur. IH still offered remote couplers at both the rear and center of the tractor if desired.

Behind the operator seat was the PTO control-valve lever. Initially IH used a straight cast-iron lever, but in order to reduce free travel and deflection, a new one-piece handle rod was released, which necessitated the use of a rubber knob. The new style one-piece PTO handle rod was released for production on F-706 SN#17200, I-706 SN#2524, F-806 SN#12713, and I-806 SN#2867 and on models that followed. The PTO unit was independent from

This left-hand side view of the 1206 Farmall Turbo diesel prototype, dated June 18, 1964, clearly shows the engine air cleaner intake stack on the left side of the hood. The pull cable, which operated an ether-assist starting canister, is located just ahead of the battery on this side. IH would later switch to an electric solenoid for reliability. *Author Collection*

In this right-hand view of the 1206 prototype, IH's RD-style diesel fuel injection pump is clearly visible. IH replaced the RD pump with a Rosa Master–brand pump prior to actual production. An alternator was now used (mounted above the injection pump) for greater reliability and larger amperage production than the previously used generator. *Author Collection*

the rest of the tractor, having its own hydraulic pump to power the hydraulically actuated multidisc clutch. Using 12 steel and 5 fiber splined discs contained in a clutch carrier, the clutch engagement piston was controlled by pressurized hydraulic oil flow from the control valve. By increasing the number of fiber discs to seven and decreasing the steel disc content to nine in the unit, a heavy-duty PTO clutch was born. IH finally made this clutch stack count change in the later production 86 series tractors during the 1970s. Any of the tractors from the 06 series to the 86 could be converted to the heavy-duty–style clutch when they were repaired, if needed.

This new PTO also had braking pistons inside it to stop the output shaft more quickly than the previous band or planetary style PTO had been able to.

The PTO brake was necessary because, as the implements powered by the PTO grew larger, and as more power was transmitted to them, the PTO would often continue coasting after it was shut off. This was a huge safety reliability issue that the brake was needed to address. Also, the brake pistons kept the PTO from "creeping" if it were in the off position and oil leakage in the control valve occurred.

To adjust the PTO engagement pressure, a service port was added to the unit below the control valve. By turning the valve either clockwise or counterclockwise, the operator could adjust the pressure for maximum PTO clutch plate life.

The two-speed PTO unit offered both 540- and 1,000-rpm speeds. Unlike the major competitor to IH (John Deere's 4010), however, the 06 series

did not require tools, nor did it need to have the output shaft reversed to achieve the desired PTO output speed. IH used one shaft for the 540- and another for the 1,000-rpm speeds. Both shafts turned when the unit was engaged. Of course, this could be very dangerous if it were not treated with respect, but IH engineers offered excellent PTO shielding for the unit. IH continued to use this PTO unit (in slightly modified form) through its final built tractors in 1985. Case-IH uses the modified IH PTO unit in its tractors even today. That is reliability!

Both the 706 and 806 offered the farmer a choice of a fixed or swinging drawbar, and also IH's time-proved Fast Hitch or now universally accepted three-point rear hitch. It was sad to see that the Fast Hitch idea IH had been so proud (and patent protective) of was finally being replaced by the industrywide accepted three-point hitch (developed by Ferguson tractor). It's also very ironic that IH chose to hold its Fast Hitch patents so closely that no other machinery manufacturer would build implements compatible with it. Competitor John Deere approached IH during the later 1950s and asked if it would license the Fast Hitch to them. Engineers at Deere were quick to realize the superior design and capabilities of the IH Fast Hitch. IH, in its blind stupidity, said no. If IH had released its Fast Hitch patents to the industry, maybe today the Fast Hitch system would be the industry norm.

The diesel-powered 706 and 806 tractors used two six-volt batteries along with a generator with an external regulator to power the tractor's electrical system. Gasoline-powered tractors used only a single 12-volt battery, but were otherwise identical. An illuminated amp warning light in the right-hand instrument cluster glowed or flashed when problems happened with the charging system. Later in Service Bulletin #S-1654, dated January 1966, IH changed to self-exciting 55 alternators with external regulators, replacing the 32-amp generator with external regulator. This was changed

The rear view of the 1206 prototype reveals the new 18.4-38 rear tires. IH worked with several tire manufacturers to develop tires that could "stay on the rim," as the technology of the time was not prepared for turbo power. Another interesting feature is the combination of the IH Fast Hitch and the new industry-adopted three-point hitch. By removing the lower link ball arms of the three-point hitch, the Fast Hitch could be used. *Author Collection*

to provide higher electrical output for the ever-increasing electrical requirements of implements and accessories.

The 706 and 806 were both available in a high-clearance version for those who needed extra ground clearance for crops grown in beds or sugar cane. These tractors were identical to their Farmall-style counterparts, except for longer front-axle spindles and the uses of rear-drive drop housings.

IH also made the 706 and 806 tractors in standard tread or International version. These tractors were designed for the open plains of the Wheat Belt. In January of 1965, IH offered an optional attachment for the I-706 and I-806 called the rear platform extension. This could be ordered on tractors not equipped with two- or three-point hitch or over-center clutch. It provided additional room for carrying farm materials such as seed sacks, and could be used for rear operator mounting, but not for extra riding passengers.

IH also offered factory-installed front-wheel assist (FWA) axle as an added cost option. The 06 series tractors installed with front-wheel assist used a drive axle made by the Coleman Mfg. Co. IH retained the use of Coleman as its FWA supplier until the 86 series was announced in 1976. Tractors that were equipped with FWA from the factory had a chrome emblem reading "All Wheel Drive" attached to the hood side. This was the same emblem IH used on its immensely popular SCOUT sport utility vehicle.

Another option that IH offered starting in January of 1965 was an enclosed operator's cab. The cab could be

The early production version of the Farmall 1206 Turbo Diesel row-crop tractor. The 1206 had only a straight exhaust pipe, not a muffler. IH used white-painted wheels, grille shell, and fenders to make the 1206 stand out. It did, as sales of the 1206 rocketed to over 8,400 tractors during the 1965 to 1967 production run. *State Historical Society of Wisconsin*

ordered either as factory or field installed for both the 706 and 806. It was built for IH by Stolper-Allen Co. of Menomonee Falls, Wisconsin, and featured an optional heater attachment along with opening side and rear windows to offer year-round operator comfort. The use of surrounding tinted safety glass helped cut down on glare. An overhead-mounted two-speed pressurized fan with a removable and reusable filtering element kept the dust out and maintained a comfortable air flow inside. The air nozzle could be rotated to direct airflow for defrosting the windshield or blowing air where the operator wanted it. By pulling a simple lever, the operator could make the fan recirculate air for faster cold weather startups. The wide opening entry door automatically cleared the rear tire by means of a cable or chain that folded the lower section up. The door could be locked wide open, if the operator so chose. The right-hand side window and rear window also opened for full ventilation. The cab offered, as optional equipment, a second rear floodlight and rear, brake-operated stoplight.

Air conditioning was added as an optional attachment to the tractor cab in late 1966. This was not the add-on unit that the competitors used, but a highly efficient large-capacity 13,200-Btu unit that made a minimal power demand. This pre-charged AC unit could be either factory installed or dealer installed on a tractor. Because it was designed specifically for the IH cab, the owner didn't need to worry about the engine overheating or changing the engine cooling system. Tractors that have the AC unit are easily identifiable by the condenser box attached to the rear of the cab roof, and the large freon compressor mounted outside the engine's right-hand side.

One often-overlooked feature that the cab offered was the safety it provided. It kept the operator away from the tractor's wheels and prevented him from falling out of the operator's seat into any PTO-driven shafts. It also made highway travel safer by keeping road debris from striking the driver. About the only thing the cab's design lacked was a roll-over protective structure (ROPS). If the tractor were to upset with a non-ROPS cab, injuries could actually be more serious.

This new cab was "just like being at home," IH salesman claimed. This author vividly remembers spending many an hour inside one of these cabs, which, due to its shape and unique folding door, had been dubbed an "Ice Cream Box" cab because of its similarity to a half-gallon box of ice cream. The tractor the author recalls was a Farmall 1206 with more than 17,000 original, untouched engine hours on it. It seemed that it really would have been quieter (and a lot cooler on 90-degree days) to ride in the engine oil pan than in that cab. But the development of the tractor

Nebraska Tractor Tests: 1963			
Model	**Fuel**	**Test No.**	**PTO Power**
Farmall 706	Gasoline	858	73.82
Farmall 706	LPG	860	73.66
Farmall 706	Diesel	856	72.42
Farmall 806	Gasoline	859	93.27
Farmall 806	LPG	861	93.42
Farmall 806	Diesel	857	94.93

The rigid frame design of the IH 4100 four-wheel drive gave the operator a choice of two- or four-wheel steering. A rear-mounted three-point hitch and PTO attachments were optional equipment. Notice the front ballast weights needed to maintain tractor balance and traction. *Author Collection*

cab meant progress. It was the first small step IH and every other tractor company would take to improve the operator's environment, and it was something that itself would be greatly improved over the next two decades.

Both the 706 and 806 were immensely popular in sales. Production numbers for the 706 Farmall ran to 46,146 units, while the International 706 had 5,487 units. The Farmall 806 was close in production with 42,957 units and 8,052 International 806 units were built during the 1963 to 1967 production run.

Big Turbo Diesel Power:
The 1206 Turbo Diesel Tractor

In August 1965, IH announced its first ever 100+ horsepower row-crop tractor, the 1206 Turbo diesel. This was the first IH row-crop tractor to be fitted with a factory-installed turbocharger unit. IH's own SOLAR division supplied the turbocharger unit for the 1206. This was big tractor power for the modern farmer. The idea of a 100+ horsepower tractor was nearly unthinkable. The majority of tractors being sold were still in the 40 to 70 horsepower range; wouldn't a 100-horsepower tractor be

too clumsy and awkward? As it proved, no.

During testing and development of the 1206, three major challenges developed. First, an engine capable of delivering 100+ horsepower had to be built. Working together with engineers from the SOLAR division of IH, designers retooled the D-361 engine (used in the 806) for heavy-duty turbocharged duty. Second, the power train needed to be beefed up to handle the extra horsepower from the turbo. The engineers at Hinsdale designed an all-new heavy-duty power train using specially hardened gears, heavier pinions and final

This rare color photo shows the IH HT-340 hydrostatic-drive gas turbine engine tractor painted blue, white, and silver, not silver and white, as the final version is today. The gas turbine never made it beyond this experimental unit, but IH expanded the hydrostatic-drive transmission to farm tractors in 1967 with the 656 Hydro. *State Historical Society of Wisconsin*

This photo of the HT-340 was taken at the Hinsdale, Illinois, engineering facility in 1961. The HT-340 was purely a concept vehicle used to test new tractor systems. The loud exhaust noise and high fuel consumption of the turbine engine was its downfall. The hydrostatic-drive transmission became a huge success for IH. The HT-340 is currently in storage at the Smithsonian Institution in Washington, D.C. *State Historical Society of Wisconsin*

The first 100+ horsepower hydrostatic-drive tractor built was the model 1026. The 1026 was only offered in hydrostatic drive. Here a 1026 is being test run at the Farmall plant on a roller treadmill. IH put all of its tractors through similar tests for quality assurance checks. *State Historical Society of Wisconsin*

drive gears (1/2 inch wider than those of the 806), a wider PTO drive gear, and bearings that could reliably deliver 98 horsepower to the drawbar. The inline shifting control used on the 806 was retained on the 1206. Third, the tires were a big problem for IH. The tires used on the tractors of the day did not even begin to hold up. The 1206 had major tire sidewall buckling—and even failure—with conventional tractor tires. Some tires spun off the rim during testing. This was a big disappointment to the engineers. IH worked with major tire manufacturers for over two years to develop a completely new kind of tire that could put the 1206's power to the ground. This was the 18.4-38 heavy-duty tire, designed to have the casing, lug strength, and wear that could stand up to the 1206.

When the 1206 was started, the engine's exhaust gases spun the turbocharger turbine at high speeds. The exhaust gas turbine was coupled to another turbine wheel that drew intake air into the engine. As more air was compressed into the engine cylinders, more fuel could be injected, with the result being an increase of horsepower. The extra intake air also helped to clean the engine combustion chambers so that the head valves, pistons, and injectors all ran cooler with a turbocharger. The turbo eliminated the need for a muffler and had better response to load changes and high-altitude operation.

Because the 1206 was turbocharged, special care was needed when hauling the tractor on trucks or by rail. Air entering the exhaust could cause the turbo to spin in a way called "windmilling." If the engine was not running, oil could not lubricate the turbo bearings causing turbo failure. To prevent this, a small spring was added to the exhaust pipe

rain cap at Farmall Works starting June 14, 1966. The spring was to be discarded upon arrival at the dealer.

The DT-361 engine was not just a turbocharged 806 engine. Instead, IH engineers built the 1206 specifically for turbo power right from the start. Using twinjet oil-cooled pistons, a bigger 10-inch dry-type air cleaner (with dual elements), an increased capacity radiator, a bigger fan, and a larger engine oil cooler, the 1206 was built from the start to handle a turbo. Something that an add-on turbo kit (which many after-marketers were selling) couldn't even begin to touch. The "Elotherm"-hardened crankshaft used seven main bearings for added strength and featured up to 100 percent stronger construction for longer wear and more strength.

IH sent Farmall 1206 tractor serial #502 to the Nebraska Tractor Test in September of 1965 for test #910. This was the first test of a turbocharged row-crop tractor with more than 100 horsepower. The 1206 recorded just over 112 maximum horsepower with a horsepower-hour-per-gallon rating of 15.95, a very good rating for a tractor of this size.

The 1206 was offered in both row-crop and standard tread versions. The basic difference was the tire choices, fenders, speeds, and axle equipment. An IH-built DT-361 turbocharged six-cylinder dry sleeve engine was the only power plant offered on the 1206. The was, however, a choice of optional equipment available to the farmer on the 1206. This included the transmission TA, wide or narrow front ends on the Farmall version along with an enclosed operator's cab, three-point Fast Hitch (combination three-point hitch and fast hitch), single speed (1,000 rpm only) PTO, dual rear wheels, and other features.

The 1206's introduction was also marked by a new rear wheel fender design. These new fenders were called the "Deluxe Fender" (Flattop fender) attachment. The Deluxe Fenders were taller, wider, and offered more protection to the operator from field debris than the shell-style fenders had. The tractor headlight was relocated from the side of the fuel tank cowling to the fender, and a

The first of a new kind of tractor for the farmer was IH's 656 hydrostatic drive. Available in both Farmall and International versions, the 656 opened the door for hydrostatic power on farms. By using a single lever the operator could control both vehicle speed and direction! Hydrostatic drives were ideally suited for front-end loader and PTO work. *Author Collection*

second field light was added for additional nighttime lighting power. These new "Deluxe" Fenders were added as optional equipment on the 706 and 806, later becoming standard equipment. It is interesting that on the early series of Deluxe Fenders, IH did not put a handgrip hole on the right-hand fender; only the left-hand fenders had the handgrip hole. Later, all Deluxe Fenders had handgrip holes in them. Today, it is rare to find an original right-hand Deluxe Fender without the handgrip hole.

The original paint scheme for the 1206 was plain IH red, with white side panels and silver rear wheel rims, just like its little brother 806. A new, welded tubular steel grille replaced the heavy and awkward-to-handle cast bar grille found on the 806. After engineering a real powerhouse for the farmer, IH decided to doll it up.

First, IH painted gleaming IH 901 white the cast-iron grille housing, the new deluxe flat-top rear fenders, and the rear wheel discs. Second, IH added a scripted gold-trimmed decal on each the side of the tractor hood that read "TURBO." The Turbo decal quickly alerted the farmer to the fact that this tractor was turbocharged powered. The Turbo decal, along with the unique white paint scheme, brought a lot of attention to the 1206. This newfound attention reaped an extra (and intentional) benefit: increased tractor sales, exactly what IH wanted.

The 1206 model identification itself was an interesting product graphic change. IH released the 1206 with a white decal on the radiator cowling stating "1206" with the word "Diesel" underneath it. This was printed as a simple, gold-border-outlined white decal. In 1966, IH replaced the decal with a metal emblem plate similar in design to those on the 706 and 806. When IH made this change, it also appeared to make some adjustments to the engine to produce more power, or at least that's how it seems. Anyone who's driven both the white (decal) 1206 and the gold (metal plate) 1206 can easily attest that the gold 1206 just has more power.

The Farmall 1206 was a good seller for IH, with more than 8,400 Farmall tractors built and another 1,589 tractors made in the standard tread International version. Not bad for a big tractor that was probably ahead of its time.

Hundreds of 1206s were put to dual use by farmers who used them for farming during the week and at local tractor pulls during the weekend. One of the better-known IH dealers to build pulling tractors was Midway Equipment Co. of Marshall, Wisconsin. At this IH dealer, many hours were spent on IH tractor-pulling R&D. One of the

A view of the working end of the I-656 Hydro. A three-point hitch, 540 rpm PTO, and dual remote hydraulic valves were available as optional equipment to tailor the 656 Hydro to the farmer's operation. Using either gasoline or diesel engines developing 63 PTO horsepower, the 656 Hydro was a bear for work but easy to drive. The first I-656 Hydro built was SN#9621, built in 1967. *Author Collection*

more humorous R&D incidents happened when a 1206 was being tested on a dynamometer. While operating at full load, the tractor gave off a load pop. It was shut down immediately to check for damage and to find the possible cause. About 30 seconds later, bystanders heard a clink, and a chunk of iron bounced off the metal shop roof and landed on the ground. It was a turbine wheel from the tractor's turbocharger. One can only guess what orbit the wheel had reached before it returned to earth.

IH's "Practical" Four-Wheel-Drive Tractor

After showing the world what it could build for the big farmer with its model 4300 tractor, IH decided it was time to build something more marketable. It hit the mark with its new model 4100 tractor.

The 4100 (and the 4300) was still made for IH by its Hough Industrial Division. Using a DT-429 turbocharged six-cylinder IH-built engine as its power plant, the 4100 cranked out over 125 drawbar and 140 PTO horsepower. A dual-element dry-type air cleaner protected the engine from harmful dirt and dust particles. Dual full flow fuel filters not only kept impurities from damaging the injection pump, but they were also vertically mounted for easy, no-mess servicing.

Using both the speed and range transmissions from the 806–1206 series tractors gave the operator a choice of four speeds in each range (high, low, reverse). The IH TA was not available on the 4100. All the transmission controls were located on the operator's right-hand side on a convenient-to-reach console. The operator could even choose between four-wheel drive for fieldwork and two-wheel drive for travel, just by moving a lever. Because the frame on the 4100 was rigid, the front axle had a built-in oscillation feature that allowed it to follow the contours of the ground. This kept all four wheels in constant contact with the ground for safe braking.

An optional 1,000-rpm-only PTO unit could be ordered as optional equipment for the rear of the tractor.

This PTO unit featured a pressure-lubricated multidisc clutch pack and had a shear coupling to protect the transmission against overload.

A padded seat with a backrest and an extension was mounted on a positioning linkage that used rubber springs and an oil-filled shock absorber to smooth out any bumps encountered in the field or road. An optional modern cab featured tinted glass and opening side and rear windows. A heater and air conditioner were optional equipment too. Insulation in the cab helped keep the cold out and noise out, allowing greater operator comfort. The cab was clean, quiet, and comfortable.

An integral 100-gallon fuel tank gave the operator the necessary fuel reserve to be able to work hard all day without stops. One could cover more ground in less time, saving wear on machinery and fuel.

A flip-open toolbox (which also served as the tractor's second step) offered a spacious safe and dry area in which to keep tools, spare implement parts, or a grease gun.

IH sent the 4100 four-wheel drive to the Nebraska Tractor Testing lab in November of 1965. Using tractor serial #502 for the test, the 4100 recorded in excess of 115 drawbar horsepower in tractor test #931. A PTO test was not performed.

There were 1,217 units of the 4100 built during its 1966 to 1968 production run. The nearly identical (except for decals) 4156 replaced the 4100 in 1969. Only 218 units of the 4156 tractor rolled off the assembly line in the model's two-year existence.

Hydrostatic Drive Reaches the Farmer: The Experimental HT-340 leads to the 656 Hydrostatic Drive Tractor

In 1959, IH engineers were working on new methods of power transmission in farm tractors. IH experimented with hydro-mechanical drive and torque converters, and an idea that had proliferated in the aircraft industry since World War II: hydrostatic drive.

The journey into tractor transmission history began with a stock I-340 Utility tractor. The first challenge that IH engineers faced was totally replacing the I-340's gear-drive transmission and final drive with a fully hydrostatic unit.

At the 1967 Farm Progress Show in Illinois, IH's display heavily featured the new hydrostatic-drive tractor. In this "ride on" display, operators could move the Speed Ratio lever and see exactly how smooth the wheels would operate through the plexiglass fender. IH was quick to capitalize on farm and trade-show exhibitions to display new products. *Author Collection*

Using off-the-shelf components from other manufacturers, IH was able to create a successful hydrostatic drive. A variable displacement Lucas-brand pump and two Staffa-brand wheel motors were the basic components of this system. This tractor was completed in 1960 and was labeled the HD-340. The HD stood for Hydrostatic Drive.

After the success of the hydrostatic transmission replacement, IH engineers decided to test a new source for tractor power generation. Instead of modifying an internal combustion engine or using exotic fuels, they opted for a total engine transplant, adapting a SOLAR T-62T gas turbine engine to the HD-340. The T-62T turbine was capable of 90-horsepower output, but the hydrostatic required only about 40 horsepower to operate effectively. The T-62T was "de-tuned" to handle the pressure in—and speed limitations of—the hydrostatic drive. The engine was 21 inches long, less than 13 inches in diameter, and weighed less than 90 pounds. The governed speed of the turbine was 57,000 rpm. Output speed from the engine was 6,000 rpm. This passed through a 3-to-1-reduction gearbox for a 2,000-rpm input to the transmission. Anything faster would overspeed the hydro pumps, causing them to burn up. The engine was air-cooled; no antifreeze or water were required. This was a very powerful, lightweight source of tractor power.

With the installation of the turbine engine, the test vehicle known as the HD-340 became the HT-340—Hydrostatic Turbine 340 tractor. The main feature of the HT-340 was its simplicity of operation. When the operator turned a key and pushed a simple start button, the engine starting was handled automatically by a control box. The control box activated the starter, opened the fuel valve at the proper engine speed, energized the turbine's spark igniter, and finally switched the starter over to a generator (much like that on a Cub Cadet) once self-sustaining engine speed was reached. Sensors protected the turbine from overspeed and high temperature meltdown.

"In IH we trust" was just one of the vows said at this wedding of Greg Nerroth and his bride, Barbara, of Antioch, Illinois. A pair of Farmall tractors made the ideal altar for this wedding. Greg, who farms 300 acres, promised to love, honor, and always use IH tractors. *Author Collection*

The gasoline engine in the HD-340 also served as a front frame structural member. A new fabricated frame was built to mount the turbine on, and the engine was forward mounted in the chassis to allow adequate area for air-intake openings. The engine's air entered through the side of the hood and exited vertically near the front. A coarse screen covering the two intake areas kept out large foreign objects. (An air filter wasn't not necessary since the turbine was relatively insensitive to dust or dirt ingestion.) The blast force of the exhaust air was enough to carry it high above the operator. Even when driving into a strong headwind, exhaust gas deflection back to the operator was nearly nonexistent. Designers retained the original wide front axle from the I-340. The light weight of the turbine engine required the addition of cast-iron weights to the front end for steering stability.

The compact size of the turbine engine offered IH engineers a chance to do some creative styling to help improve

forward visibility. They located the tractor's fuel tank behind the operator (a design IH would later return to in the 86 series), and had indents cut into it to facilitate the operation of the tractor's Fast Hitch. The tank was reshaped for better rearward visibility as well. This new industrial design practice was widely applied to tractor designs of the 1980s and 1990s.

IH shocked the world in 1961 with the announcement and public showing of the futuristically styled HT-340 tractor. The first public showing of the HT-340 came at the University of Nebraska's 10th annual Tractor Day in Lincoln, on July 20, 1961. After that show, the HT-340 suffered some major damage when the truck hauling it overturned in Missouri, sending the HT-340 back to Hinsdale for repairs.

After the HT-340's last public operation in 1962, the tractor had its batteries removed and its hydrostatic oil drained, and it required major maintenance to keep it in operating condition. It was never shown again (except for the open house at Farmall Works) until its retirement party.

IH officially retired the HT-340 tractor at a May 25, 1967, press conference, permanently lending it to the Smithsonian Institution in Washington, D.C. Its first duty there was to be part of a display honoring the 75th anniversary of the gasoline-powered farm tractor during September and October 1967. The HT-340, along with an 1892 Froelich (early forerunner of the Deere tractor line) and a 1918 Fordson, was put on special display in the Museum of History and Technology in Washington, D.C.

The concepts tested and proven in the HT-340 did actually reach the farmer. The turbine engine was practically abandoned as a power source alternative due to its relatively loud engine noise levels and high fuel consumption. The hydrostatic-drive transmission proved to be a success that did reach the "practical world."

IH unveiled the first practical hydrostatic-drive transmission farm tractor in the summer of 1967 with the release of the 656 hydrostatic-drive tractor. Now the farmer had a choice of gasoline-, diesel-, or LPG-powered fully automatic, clutchless, gearless, clash-free shifting tractor operation. The 656 was offered in both row-crop (Farmall) and standard utility tread (International) versions. The 656 hydrostatic Farmall (test #967) and International (test #968) were both tested at the Nebraska Tractor Test lab from October 31 through November 29, 1967. Both tractors produced about 62 PTO horsepower.

The 656 Hydro was unique in that the operator controlled the tractor's speed and travel direction simply by moving a single lever. This proved to be the ideal tractor for front-end loader applications and farm tasks that required a constant field speed regardless of load. Hay baling was an ideal example of an operation in which a hydro tractor could outperform a gear drive. When the baler encountered a slug, the tractor operator simply pulled the lever back, slowing the machine ground speed while retaining full PTO speed.

Quickly realizing the sales potential of hydrostatic-drive tractors, IH added more models to the hydro lineup. In 1968, IH introduced its second farm tractor with hydrostatic drive, the model 544. Like the 656 tractor, the 544 was offered in hydrostatic drive in both the row-crop (Farmall) and standard (International) style versions. The 544 used either a C-200 gasoline engine or a D-239 diesel engine as its power source. Both of these four-cylinder engines were dynamically balanced, so they ran as smoothly as a six-cylinder. The 544 developed about 54 PTO horsepower. Both the 544 and 656 remained in the IH tractor lineup until 1973, when the 666 and 666 Hydro replaced both models. The reason these two models were retained that long was that their sales continued to make them very profitable to produce for IH. If IH had dropped them, it would have lost market share.

The 826 hydrostatic-drive tractor was rated at 84 PTO horsepower. Using either a German-built D358 six-cylinder naturally aspirated diesel engine or a C-301 IH-built gasoline engine, the 826 Hydro was the perfect choice for those who needed hydro power in a midsized tractor. The 826 and 1026 hydrostatic drives were tractors made for larger farms.

In 1969, IH introduced the first ever 100+ horsepower hydrostatic model, which it called the 1026. Using a DT-407 engine, the 1026 delivered 112 PTO horsepower for the big farmer who needed hydrostatic drive. The 1026 was made exclusively as a hydrostatic-drive model. A gear-drive version of the 1026 was never made, unlike the other hydro-drive tractors. The optional equipment for the 1026 was similar to the 56 series gear-drive tractors, with the exception of

In this photo dated April 11,1966, IH reveals its replacement for the model 706, the new 756. While still retaining the D-310 diesel engine built in Neuss, Germany, the 756 had an improved H pattern shifting layout. Notice the uniquely shaped shifting levers and the very prototypical 756-emblem medallion, both of which were changed for the final production version. IH also outfitted this prototype 756 with a hydraulic suspension seat. *Author Collection*

a TA not being offered. The 1026 actually had some of the lowest production numbers IH ever developed, with only 2,414 Farmall units and 58 International (standard) version units. This surely places the I-1026 among the rarest IH tractors ever made.

The design of the hydrostatic-drive transmission relied on pressurized hydraulic oil to allow its movement. When the engine was shut off, the tractor couldn't move. This made pull-starting a hydro tractor impossible. The hydraulically engaged TA tractors also had this characteristic. To allow some movement with the engine off or "inching" back up to implements, an "inching" pedal was added at the spot where the clutch pedal is located on the gear-drive models. By depressing this pedal, the operator could control the hydro precisely in tight situations or make emergency stops.

A very important maintenance item on hydrostatic-drive tractors is the changing of the hydro oil and filters. Failure to regularly change both would lead to premature wear and possible hydro failure. This author has serviced many hydro tractors, with the most memorable one being a one-owner Hydro 70 whose owner religiously changed filters and added Hy-Tran oil every year. Eventually the tractor began to slip. After teardown, the hydro charge pump proved to be scored, requiring a repair costing several thousand dollars. The oil drained from the machine was clear like water, not caramel color, like oil is. The tractor didn't fail due to filter neglect; the oil had simply been topped off but never changed since it had been new,

Using a D-407 IH-built six-cylinder naturally aspirated diesel engine, the 856 was rated at 100 PTO horsepower. When the 856 was introduced in 1967, wide front ends were quickly gaining acceptance. They offered high front load carrying capability and better stability. This 856 is outfitted with an optional belly-mounted fuel tank. This gave the operator nearly twice the operating range and yet did not compromise tractor clearance. *Author Collection*

and it was worn out. If you change filters, change the oil, too.

Another hydro story involves a 186 hydro tractor that failed to drive in forward. IH designed the hydro servo control valve to have two relief valves, one for each direction of travel. By switching valves, the tractor could at least be moved safely to a repair facility.

IH assembled its hydrostatic-drive transmissions in a place called the "white

room" at the Farmall Works. In this temperature- and dust-controlled "clean" room, the precision components of the hydrostatics could be assembled safely. Hydrostatic components were manufactured with incredibly precise machining tolerances. These tight tolerances were needed to keep the pressurized oil contained. An additional hydraulic oil filter was added to hydrostatic tractors that had a higher micron rating. The micron rating is the measurement of how tiny a particle would have to be to pass through the filtering media. Even the tiniest dirt particles can quickly destroy the precision-made hydraulic pumps and motors. When the basic hydro transmission section is fully assembled, it is then wrapped and sealed before being sent to the final assembly line to be mated with a final drive and engine.

While IH was busy putting hydrostatics in its farm tractors, another use

Nebraska Tractor Tests: 1967-1970

Model	Fuel	Test No.	PTO Power
Farmall 544 Hydro	Gasoline	1007	53.87
Farmall 544 Hydro	Diesel	1029	55.52
Farmall 656 Hydro	Diesel	967	66.06
Farmall 656 Hydro	Gasoline	968	65.80
Farmall 826 Hydro	Diesel	1046	84.66
Farmall 1026 Hydro	Diesel	1047	112.45

An IH 756 with a four-bottom fully mounted moldboard plow. The white-colored cylinders on the plow are actually covers for the large trip springs that would be activated if a rock or obstruction was incurred. IH produced more than 20,000 of the 756 tractors from 1967 to 1971. *State Historical Society of Wisconsin*

for hydropower was found: the Cub Cadet. IH released the first-ever hydro-static-drive garden tractor in the model 123 Cub Cadet in 1967. The hydrostatic-drive feature proved so successful that even today every major lawn power equipment manufacturer builds a hydrostatic-drive machine.

Refinement of Power: The IH 56 and 26 Series

In 1967, IH announced the replacement series for the 06 tractors. These new tractors were called the 56 series. The 656 replaced the 606, the 756, the 706; the 856, the 806; and the 1256, the 1206. A new tubular steel grille (similar to that on the 1206) and revised grille housing were the striking features of the 56 series.

The 656 was basically unchanged except for the grille being switched from a mesh screen, like the 706 used, to a tubular bar style. Also the metal emblem plate on the hood side was switched from "Farmall" to "International." This gave the 656 what was called "family styling." The 756 still retained the D-310 diesel and C-291 gasoline engines as

its power plants. The 856 and 1256 both used the new D-407 (856) or DT-407 (1256) instead of the DT-361, as the 806 and 1206 had. The 407 engine was basically a modified 361 with a larger bore and stroke. The D-310 diesel engines now featured a spin-on-style dual element fuel filter.

The use of 55-amp alternators with external regulators was standard equipment on the 56 series tractors. The diesel-powered models still used two six-volt batteries linked in series, while the gasoline tractors had a single 12-volt battery.

The 756 was offered in Farmall (row-crop) International (standard) and Hi-Clearance configurations. The 856 was also offered in these three styles, along with a Wheat Land tractor version being made too. The Wheat Land version differed from the standard version in that two auxiliary hydraulic rear outlets with check valves were standard equipment along with a platform extension and a fixed-height heavy-duty swinging drawbar. The only optional equipment was an operator cab and heater, dual rear wheels, and front and

rear weights. The 856 Wheat Land was a package tractor aimed particularly at the Wheat Belt market. IH hoped that the lower-priced 856 Wheat Land tractor would switch some customers to IH from the 5020 John Deere.

IH offered the 1256 in Farmall and International versions only. A Hi-Clearance model was not available.

With the increased horsepower farmers were demanding from tractors, IH needed a better way to fasten the rear wheel to the axle. The old method of relying on a cast-iron block keyed to fit the axle and retained by two fine-threaded bolts was not working. Even using these blocks in tandem was not the answer. IH needed a new design to keep its tractor's wheels on.

So was born the IH "wedge-lock" wheel design. This new design used a single screw bolt to tighten or loosen the wheel wedge, locking it to the axle. This single bolt design made wheel tread changes simpler and faster. Each wheel had two wedges connected by a single cap screw. The operator installed two wedge rods in the wheel and then turned the bolt to loosen the wedge.

When the first wedge contacted the wedge rod, the remaining wedge was forced loose from the axle. When both wedges were loose, the wheel could be moved on the axle. To tighten the wheels, the procedure was just reversed.

The wedge-lock wheels were an extra-heavy cast design. So much, in fact, that an operator might find he needed to use one fewer set of wheel weights. The new wedge-lock wheels were an optional field-installed attachment on the 706, 806, and 1206 tractors. Wedge-lock wheels were standard equipment on the 856, 1026, 1256, and were later introduced on the 1456. They were optional equipment on the 826 tractor.

One area that had plagued IH in the 06 series was the shifting controls. More specifically, the Range lever. The inline shifting found on the 06, where the operator had to shift past low range to get to high range, was changed to an H layout shifting pattern. Neutral was in the center, low was straight down, high was straight up, and reverse was located by moving the lever to the right and down. There was no more grinding of range gears to get to reverse, something that many farmers had complained of when using a front loader. The four-speed control lever design remained basically unchanged, except that both shifting levers and the TA lever were now tubular chrome-plated steel with rubber grips instead of the cast-metal design used on the 06 series. A small light illuminated the shifting levers during nighttime use.

The "new" IH-built D-407 and DT-407 models replaced the reliable D-361 and DT-361 diesel engines as the main line power sources for the 56 series. Larger engine oil coolers and the use of Schwitzer-brand turbochargers (replacing the IH Solar turbo) were the main differences. A model 3LD279 turbocharger was

The Farmall 544 was available in either gasoline- or diesel-powered versions. Sales of the 544 to larger fleet users proved so successful that IH kept the 544 in its tractor lineup from 1968 to 1973, with over 13,000 tractors being built. *State Historical Society of Wisconsin*

Here is the first of 410 specially labeled IH 656 tractors that were sold to the Chilean government. These 656s, along with a fleet of IH implements, were to be distributed to farmers in the most remote areas of Chile for intense development of agriculture. This photo, dated April 30, 1969, proves that the name "International Harvester" was not just a catch phrase; IH was truly international. *Author Collection*

used on the DT-407. Later, in 1971, IH replaced the service parts of the 3LD279 turbo with the 3LD229 for improved performance.

The use of the Rosa Master-style injection pump was continued in the 407 engine. One major change to the fuel system was the replacement of the cartridge-style fuel filters with new spin-on–style fuel filters. These new spin-on filters were still vertically mounted, but much easier for the operator to service—just spin off the old filters and spin on the new.

Operator convenience was becoming more important; for instance, such features as a new tilting steering wheel became optional equipment. The wheel could now be adjusted to the angle the operator needed whether he was seated or standing. A new high-back seat with folding armrests and a hydraulic seat

suspension was standard equipment. This seat raised or lowered to any height hydraulically with fingertip control. The seat slid fore and aft for more legroom, and could be tilted for comfort, too. The use of a seamless, heavily upholstered fabric made the seat rainproof.

Factory-installed operator cab enclosures were quickly gaining in popularity. IH was still using its single-door "Ice Cream Box" cab on the 56 series it had offered on the 06 series. In 1970 it offered a new two-door cab called the Deluxe Cab. This cab was built by Excel Industries of Hesston, Kansas, and still offered the owner a heater and the choice of an optional air conditioner. Wide-angled entry steps made cab entry and exit a breeze. For those who did not need the comfort of an enclosed cab, IH began offering a factory-installed two-post ROPS on the 656, 756,

Where is the best place to get IH parts and service? Your IH dealer, of course! This 1968 photo shows the newly opened IH store in Burlington, Wisconsin (now called Otters Sales & Service), managed by Harry Otter. This dealership is still very much alive and well yet today. The signage has been updated, but the building is basically unchanged. Pay close attention to the white-painted demonstrator baler at the far left. *Author collection*

856, and 1256 starting in 1967. A sun-shade canopy top was also optional to give the operator a shaded work area.

The tractor industry was becoming much more safety conscious. IH had, since the 06 series, used a safety starting switch on the clutch pedal. The switch was activated when the clutch was depressed before starting. Not every operator agreed on the necessity of this and in several instances when the safety starting switch was bypassed and the tractor was started while in gear, people were run over, seriously hurt, and even killed. Today tractor manufacturers install elaborate safety starting systems to protect the operator and others from death or injury.

During a field demo day sponsored by IH in northeastern Wisconsin, an important lesson in tractor tires was demonstrated. Using four identically prepared 856 tractors (two pulling identical-sized plows, and the other two pulling identical-sized disk harrows) in the same field under the same conditions (operating in

the same gears, too), it was proved that bigger is not always better.

Two of the 856s were outfitted with 18.4-38–size rear tires, while the other pair of 856s had 18.4-34 tires. In the lighter soils both tractors performed equally well. Neither one outdid the other. When they encountered hard clay or heavy draft loads, however, the 856s with 18.4-34 rear tires just walked away from the pair of 856s using 18.4-38 tires. The reason for this can be explained in one word: torque. By having the tractor's rear axle closer to the ground, more torque could be applied to the wheels, thus putting more engine power to the ground. Since the 18.4-34s are lower to the ground than the 18.4-38s, torque transfer is higher. This was similar to the lesson IH learned while developing the 1206. The 1206 had more torque than the tires could absorb, causing tire sidewall failure.

Earlier that same year, IH had 856s (ironically) on field demo at the Farm Progress Show. These tractors were

pulling moldboard plows in a field demo plot along with some Oliver and Allis-Chalmers tractors and plows. The 856s seemed to lag further and further behind the competition in the field. IH field reps were at a loss to determine the cause of the problem. All of the tractors used the same fuel and pulled the same-sized plows in the same field; conditions were equal. What could be the problem? An alert IH dealership mechanic had the solution and asked everyone to leave the area while he got a steel fence post and fixed the 856s. He accomplished the repair by climbing atop the hood and jamming the steel post inside the muffler, breaking the internal baffle. The 856s were experiencing too much back pressure on the exhaust, causing the poor performance. After the "fix" the 856s worked much better.

Another problem that IH had in all of the 706-806-1206 series and also the early 756-856-1256 series involved the rear axles. While this was not as widespread as the 60 series final drive

Billed as the largest IH row-crop tractor made yet, the 1456 IH was only built for three years (1969 to 1971) until the new 1466 replaced it. The 1466 used larger final drive gears and brakes to tame the 131 PTO horsepower the DT407 produced. IH was busy improving the tractor cabs for the operator, too. This two-door Custom cab was outfitted with air conditioning to keep the driver cool on hot summer days. The optional belly-mounted fuel tank gave the tractor plenty of capacity to plow all day and well into the night without stopping. *State Historical Society of Wisconsin*

problem was, it was still serious. When the hydraulic oil was drained from the rear end of the 06 or 56 series, not all of it drained. The rear axle housings had their own oil level check and drain plugs, and if the drain plugs were not removed, the oil in the axle cavity could not be changed, and became trapped in the axle housing. Filling the tractor with hydraulic oil was not the problem because, after filling the Range and Speed housings, the oil level would spill over into the axle housings and fill them, too. Sometimes the operator would check the oil level in the axle housings, other times he might forget. IH was experiencing some inner axle bearing failures due to this.

To correct this problem, IH added two cored holes to the rear frame casting to allow oil circulation between the rear axle carriers and the rear frame. This also eliminated the need to check

the rear axle housing oil level. This change took place on January 29, 1969, on the following tractors: F-856 SN#20239, I-856 SN#9163, F-1256 SN#13456, I-1256 SN#8518, and F-756 SN#14318 and above. The I-756 was changed on February 3, 1969, with SN#8201 and above. IH increased the size of these core holes in the later 66 and 86 series to over 1 inch in diameter.

This author has repaired many 06 series tractors and always installs the non-mandatory IH field update to the rear frame whenever possible. To accomplish this, one must drain the hydraulic oil from the tractor and remove both axle housings. Then using a 1/2-inch drill bit (or larger), drill two holes at the lowest point of the rear frame between the cast reinforcing webbing. A large expansion plug behind the inner axle-bearing race should also be removed. Clean all metal shavings from

the housing and reassemble. The tractor is now updated and can be expected to operate smoothly for many more years.

"Operation Take Over"

This was not the code name for a CIA covert operation; instead, it was IH's tractor comparison program for 1968. In this program, the IH dealer was given an in-depth brochure featuring the specifications of the IH and competitive makes along its farm tractor line. The competitions' weak points were listed to help the dealer sales force overcome any objection or answer questions the customer might have. The new hydrostatic-drive 656 tractor was the primary demo objective of this program, but all IH tractor models were to be aggressively sold. IH was always very generous in supplying its dealers with competitive-make comparisons. This gave the dealer, in a simple book

Tractors for "Cheap" Customers

IH's main competitor (John Deere) started a tractor price war with the introduction of its model 4000 tractor. The 4000 was a no-frills, stripped-down (available with very few options), price-sensitive tractor. With a list price of about $9,000, the 4000 was the poor man's 4020.

Not to let Deere get a part of the "poor man's" market, IH introduced its economy model 856 tractor called the Custom. The 856 Custom had the same features as the regular 856 Farmall, except for a smaller fuel tank, the availability of only a single remote hydraulic valve (not two), single fender-mounted headlights, the inclusion of TA as standard equipment, and a smaller air filter element. This was big power at a low price. The sales of 856 Customs took off—so well, in fact, that IH announced the little brother to the 856 Custom a few months later: the Farmall 756 Custom, similarly equipped with features. Ironically, after the 756-856 Custom program, IH did not have another true price-sensitive tractor until the 786 was announced in 1980. Due to the short production run of the 756 and 856 Custom tractors, they are not commonly found on farms today.

In 1969, IH introduced the new model 1456 Turbo diesel tractor. This was the most powerful IH row-crop tractor made to date. It featured an improved model DT 407, six-cylinder, dry sleeve-type, turbocharged diesel engine. An optional electric air cleaner indicator was available to warn the tractor operator when air filter service was needed. A new operator's cab called the Custom Cab was built for IH by Excel Co. of Hesston, Kansas. This optional cab had two doors for easy entry or exit from either side of the tractor. This basic two-door cab design was a trademark IH kept until the very end of its tractor production. The 1456 was available as a row-crop model (Farmall), Standard tread (also called Wheat Land), and industrial versions.

During June of 1970, IH had the 1456 tested at Nebraska. Test #1048 revealed that the 1456 produced 131.8 PTO horsepower, with a fuel economy rating of 15.81 horsepower hours per gallon. This was one of the highest rated IH tractors tested at Nebraska.

To handle the increased horsepower of this new tractor, IH reengineered the tractor from grille to draw bar. Designers enlarged the radiator and moved it forward to make space for a larger engine-cooling fan. The gears in the transmission and final drives were widened and beefed up. New, heavier brakes with a larger disc diameter of over 11 inches replaced the previously used 8-inch discs. Larger bull pinion shafts along with heavier final drive axles and bearings were developed. The rear axles were now a whopping 3.5 inches in diameter.

The 1456 used a 13-51 tooth-ring gear/pinion set in its final drive. The 1206 and 1256 had used a 12-49 tooth-ring gear pinion set. When the 1206 or 1256 needed this part serviced, the 1456 parts were to be used. Because of the higher speed of the 1456 gear set (a 4.4 percent increase in speed), a 1206 or 1256 would be faster than it originally was. If two tractors were raced and one had the high-speed gear set, it would easily win.

The 1456 replaced the model 1256, which was dropped from the IH tractor lineup. The 1456 saw 5,582 Farmall units and just 294 of the International (standard) units manufactured during its short three-year production run from 1969 to 1971.

Going South of the Border

After building the 756 tractor for over five years in America, IH sent them south of the border to Mexico for another multiyear production run. Initially, IH built skidded units to its Mexican assembly facility, where the tractors were finished with the addition of wheels, tires, and other pieces. By shipping the units into Mexico as an unfinished product, IH saved millions in import/export taxes. IH would often take its old tooling from the United States and ship it to other foreign assembly plants in Mexico or Australia for one more run. The units assembled in Australia had a special AU decal applied to them to signify their point of origin.

Ever wonder how IH photographers get those great action shots? Here's an aerial view of a way to do that. The cameraman, in a special platform basket high atop an IH forklift, gets ready to zoom in and shoot the final photo. IH photographers took hundreds of photos to have the selection needed to get the right look for the ad. *Author Collection*

Chapter 3
The 1970s
POWER AND COMFORT
ARE REDEFINED

The 1970s showcased some of IH's best tractor engineering concepts ever. Operator comfort and advancements in hydraulics led the way. IH changed the way tractors were designed altogether this decade, and set new levels of operator comfort and convenience that the competition used as a benchmark. The dealer network of IH was shrinking, along with the number of farms in the United States. IH reintroduced a new dealer standards program called XL and even bring computer technology into the mainstream of farming, where it would play a major role starting that decade. By the end of the decade, however, a crippling labor strike was only the first sign of even tougher times to come in the 1980s.

The IH Gold Demonstrator Tractor Program

The summer of 1970 saw IH announce the Golden Demonstrator Tractor program to IH dealers. Through the use of specially painted IH tractors, IH dealers demonstrated the features of the IH tractor line to their customers. The main reason for the Gold Demo program was to promote the sales of the IH hydrostatic-drive tractor line. IH used production tractors and added gold-painted hoods and fenders to them. A simple black decal stating

Demonstrator was placed on the side of the tractor's hood. IH hoped that the unique gold paint scheme would draw the attention of potential customers to the dealer's lot.

In a full-page color advertisement (found in the Summer 1970 *IH FARM* magazine), IH made its potential demo customers aware of this program by stating, "In the coming months of 1970, International Harvester dealers will be undertaking the biggest farm tractor demonstration program ever! There'll be new Red and Gold demonstrators—a new 1456 turbo. . . 826 diesel, or a Hydrostatic tractor for you to test on your own fields. So watch for the Red and Gold—your chance to get the feel of modern, productive power." The advertisement had a full color photo of a 1456 Farmall equipped with two-post ROPS and canopy, shown in the red-and gold-painted demo scheme.

IH painted the 544, 656, 826, 1026, and 1456 tractors as "Gold Demos." With the exception of the 1456, all the others were available either in both gear-drive and hydrostatic-drive transmissions, or in hydrostatic drive only (1026). The 756 was not offered as a Gold Demo tractor. The demo program had two main objectives:

1. To promote the sale of IH hydrostatic drive tractors.

Using a turbocharged and intercooled DT-466 IH diesel engine, the 4386 was styled similarly to the 86 series tractors. Dual wheels all around were common on four-wheel drives for extra traction and flotation. The 4386 was still built at Steiger in Fargo, North Dakota. IH owned a 28 percent stock share of Steiger. *Author Collection*

A very rare color photo of an IH 1456 Golden Demonstrator tractor. IH used special gold-painted tractors in its 1970 Gold Demo program to draw attention to its tractor line. IH dealers were to use this special gold-painted tractor for on-farm demonstrations with the intent of boosting sales. Hydrostatic-drive tractors were especially favored for Gold Demos. IH built 544, 656, 826, 1026, and 1456 Gold Demos. Today Gold Demo tractors are highly collectible. *State Historical Society of Wisconsin*

2. To sell the new model 1456 tractor.

One trick that IH used (and very few people know about) is that some 1456 Gold Demos came equipped, from the factory, with the injection pump and injectors from a DT-429 engine. This gave the 1456s a little extra pep, and thus if a non-demo 1456 was purchased after a Gold Demo test drive, the tractor might seem a bit sluggish. Every tractor manufacturer that conducts demonstrations has built "hot" demonstrator tractors to help them get sales. Many tractor manufacturers still do this today.

Finding an original painted IH Gold Demonstrator tractor today is rare, as the tractors were to be re-painted IH red after the tractor was sold or the demo program was over. A large number of repainted IH Gold Demos are still in use today with many of the tractors, owners not realizing what they have unless the gold paint is dis-

covered. There is not a certain serial number sequence on the Gold Demos that can be used to identify a possible tractor. The only criterion that can be used right now is that the tractor must be a 1970-year model.

One point that most people didn't realize at the time of the Gold Demo program was that IH was also clearing out the factory and dealers' lots of its inventory of 56 and 26 series tractors. This was to make room for the introduction of an all-new tractor series in 1971, the IH 66 series.

A New World of Small Tractors

In 1971, IH made a bold move with the introduction of the 54 and 74 series utility tractors, part of a totally new engineered tractor line designed for worldwide sales. These new tractors were built at IH's factory in Doncaster, England. One basic tractor model was

built and then minor changes would be added for safety regulations and related equipment in each country it was sold in. The new models in this series were the 32 PTO horsepower model 354 tractor, the 40 PTO horsepower model 454 tractor, and finally the big 52 PTO horsepower model 574 tractor. All three tractors came with either gasoline- or diesel-powered engines.

The 354 tractor had such features as
- Three-point hitch with draft control
- Dry-type air cleaner
- A 144-ci engine delivering 32 PTO horsepower
- A big 12-gallon fuel tank for extra long work days
- Disc brakes, along with eight forward and two reverse speeds to allow the speeds and control needed in the field or on the road
- New sheet-metal styling that was similar to the bigger brother 66 series

Optional equipment on the 354 included auxiliary hydraulic valves, vertical exhaust, power steering, and a four-post cage-style ROPS protective frame.

Models 454 and 574 were also packed with new features. These two tractors featured draft control for smooth hitch action, with torsion bar sensing for accurate, quick-hitch sensing. The contoured, rear-mounted fuel tank put weight where it was needed—on the drive wheels for added traction—and still gave good rearward visibility. With the fuel tank moved to the rear, the operator now sat ahead of the rear axle for a smoother ride with better forward visibility.

A swept-back front axle allowed a shorter turning radius to help in tight spots or when using a front-mounted loader. Oil bathed, hydraulically actuated wet multiple disc brakes made stopping easy. Full instrumentation kept the operator aware of all the tractor's vital functions: Fuel gauge, amp gauge, oil pressure gauge, and ammeter gauge, along with warning lights, alerted you if there was a problem.

A new power shift–independent PTO with dual 540- and 1000-rpm shafts meant no oil mess to change shafts or

Multipurpose is one description of the new IH 54 series tractors. Not only are they ideal for the barnyard, but fieldwork, too. This IH 54 series is at work chopping corn silage on this bright fall day. *State Historical Society of Wisconsin*

PTO speeds. The eight forward and four reverse shift on-the-go synchronized transmission meant smooth operation. The transmission was pressure lubricated. A compact planetary final drive was inboard mounted for maximum wheel tread adjustments. The all-new "Lightning Flash" shifting pattern offered straight-line speed changes. The transmission controls were on the operator's left side, while the hitch and hydraulic controls were on the right console. This split-deck design freed up the operator from the one-arm "Octopus" operation that the competitors featured on their tractors. A deeply padded operator's seat offered all the comforts of home and then some. An adjustable seat suspension allowed the operator to adjust the seat to fit his height and weight for the perfect ride.

Maintenance was easy with the new 54 and 74 series tractors. The use of vertically mounted full flow spin-on–type oil and fuel filters made engine service a snap, even if a front-mounted loader was attached. The hydraulic filter was mounted under the right rear foot platform and was easily changed by removing a single bolt. A dipstick by the operator's feet allowed for a quick check of the hydraulic fluid level. A toolbox with ample room for tools and a grease gun or operator's manual to be stored was neatly hidden under the left-foot floorboard. Should the tractor battery, air filter, or fuse block need service, they could easily be exposed by removing a fiberglass hood center panel with a simple turn of two thumbscrews.

One of the more rare IH tractors made was the 664 model, which was introduced in 1972 and built through 1974. The 664 was created as a stopgap

The 39 PTO horsepower model 364 tractor was ideally suited for the need of any farmer, big or small. A 540-rpm rear PTO and three-point rear hitch with draft control gave the 364 the equipment to tackle almost anything you could think of. IH produced the 364 from 1976 to 1977 in a diesel engine version only. *Author Collection*

to give IH a 61-horsepower utility tractor to sell until the new 62-horsepower "worldwide" 674 series could be introduced in 1974. IH had dropped the 55-horsepower model 544 and needed a temporary replacement.

The 664 was basically a combination 656 and 674. It used the basic drivetrain from the 656 and the D-239 four-cylinder German diesel engine from the forthcoming 674. The original plans

were to call this tractor the 644, but with the 44 series being dropped and the 74 series coming out, IH changed the model number to the 664. Due to the fact that this was a fill-in tractor, IH did not test it at Nebraska.

The 664 had all the features you needed in a tractor at an inflation-fighting price—about $7,400. This was only a few hundred dollars more than the 656 cost. When the 674 was released,

however, its list price of $11,000+ made the 664 look like a bargain.

An optional category II rear three-point hitch with lower link draft torsion bar draft sensing was fast, accurate, and dependable; it was a time-proved design that got more work done. Controls for remote hydraulic valves were placed beside the seat within fingertip reach. The hydraulic system also powered the fully hydrostatic power-steering system. A swept-back front axle meant that tight turns in small work areas became a reality, not just a possibility, as with other makes of tractors.

The optional rear PTO attachment provided either 540- or 1,000-rpm PTO power. A single lever to the left of the operator controlled the fully independent PTO, and a self-contained hydraulic gear pump powered the multiple disc clutch pack.

Nebrasks Tractor Tests: 1972			
Model	**Fuel**	**Test No.**	**PTO Power**
I-454	Gasoline	1096	40.86
I-454	Diesel	1097	40.47
I-574	Gasoline	1098	52.97
I-574	Diesel	1099	52.55

A family shot of the IH utility tractor lineup of 1973. Shown (L-R) is the 61-horsepower model 674, the 44-horsepower model 454, and the 52-horsepower model 574. All three had features such as synchronized transmissions, power steering, and large-capacity rear-mounted fuel tank. *Author Collection*

Transmission controls were also easy to reach. The cowl-mounted speed-shifting lever provided five forward and one reverse speed. When the 664 was equipped with the optional TA, the number of operating speeds doubled to 10 forward and 2 reverse. By placing both the shifting and TA control levers on the cowl side, designers left the foot and knee areas uncluttered for easy entry and exit. A big 11-inch Dyna-Life drive clutch was built to take the rigorous loads that utility tractors are put to, and helped deliver the brawny power from the four-cylinder direct-injection diesel engine to the drawbar.

A padded sliding seat with backrest provided comfort while driving the 664. An optional ROPS frame with canopy was available as optional equipment for operator protection.

New Power for the Modern Farmer: The IH 66 Series Tractors

IH unveiled the all-new 66 series tractor line to the farmer in the fall of 1971. The 66 series still had the reliable IH drivetrain design of the 56 series gear and 26 series hydrostatic drives, but was powered by a totally new diesel engine.

A new wider hood and redesigned grille housing were to become the IH standard of tractor design for this decade. In the advertisement announcing the 66 series, IH was determined to make it the "totally new tractor line of tractors in ten years." The 66 series wasn't completely new, but IH made some major improvements.

"A man can spend a third of his working life on his tractor. That's a lot of time in one place . . . . We were determined to make them better places to work," said the IH introductory literature

on the new 66 series. The series offered a prelude to the all-new IH tractor operator cab, and it was loaded with many new innovative features designed to make the farmer more productive in the field.

The dual-stage dry-type air cleaner was equipped with an automatic dust unloader and an electric service indicator to avoid damage from neglect. IH was quick to replace the originally specified Donaldson-brand air filters on the 1066, 1466, and 1468 tractors with new air cleaner assemblies made by the Air Maze Company. The Air Maze filters offered greater dust capacity and helped IH overcome the objections of offering a common air filter for the 66 series. The 766 and 966 still used the Donaldson-brand of air filter assembly.

The IH-designed Dyna-Life drive clutches (available in 12-inch diameters

Nebrasks Tractor Tests: 1971-1972			
Model	**Engine**	**Test No.**	**PTO Power**
766	C-291 Gas	1094	79.73
766	D-360 Diesel	1117	85.45
966	D-414 Diesel	1082	96.01
966 Hydro	D-414 Diesel	1095	91.38
1066	DT-414 Diesel	1081	116.23
1066 Hydro	DT-414 Diesel	1083	113.58
1466	DT-436 Diesel	1080	133.40
1468 V-8	DV-550 V-8 Diesel	1118	145.49

on the 766 and 966, or 14-inch diameters on the 1066 and 1466) were retained in the 66 series. These clutches have been field proven to last longer than other types of dry clutches, delivering engine power flawlessly to the IH-built transmissions. The standard eight forward and four reverse speed transmission could be equipped with the optional "shift on the go" TA, giving 16 forward and 8 reverse speeds. Infinite speed control was available on the 966 and 1066 hydrostatic-drive tractors. An optional (except 1466) rear differential drive lock was electrically operated via a floor-mounted foot switch, to avoid spinouts.

The 66 series still offered two basic model designs: the standard tread (International) and the row-crop (Farmall). Optional FWA (made by the Coleman Manufacturing Co.) was available in either the Farmall or International version. The 766, 966, and 1066 were also available as Hi-Clearance Farmall models. The high-clearance tractors were used in areas requiring extra ground clearance, such as bedded and vine crops.

IH built a heavier, larger diameter, wide front-axle tube on the 66 series. The wide front end used on the previous 06 and 56 series was susceptible to breakage when overloaded, abused, or overextended. IH also beefed up the front bolster casting and used wider frame rails to tie the tractor together. The heavier front-end design of the 66 series helped support the extra loads that frame-mounted chemical and NH3 tanks have. Another problem that IH fixed in the 66 series was the spindle arms. The older wide front axles had a spindle arm that used a bolt to clamp it to the spindle. Over time the bolt would loosen and the arm could break, causing loss of steering control. The new front axle used a snap ring and threaded nut to hold the arm tight.

The use of "idiot lights" (like those in prior series) to warn the operator of a possible tractor problem were discontinued on the 66 series. Instead, gauges replaced the lights so the operator was aware of the machine's performance. Better forward and rearward lighting was standard on the 66 series. This made nighttime work "seem like daytime" to the operator. IH continued to use dual six-volt batteries for starting on the diesel-powered models. Gasoline-powered tractors used only a single 12-volt battery. The uses of alternators with external regulator were carried over from the 56 series.

A fully independent PTO, like the previous 56 series used, was also standard. A 540- and 1,000-rpm dual-shaft PTO unit was standard on the 966 and 1066. The 1466 had a 1,000-rpm PTO only.

The IH 66 series still used three basic hydraulic pumps to perform three separate functions. A 12 gallons-per-minute (GPM) pump served the hitch and auxiliary valves only. The MCV pump was rated at 9 GPM, and supplied the brakes, steering, TA, differential lock, pressure lubrication of the transmission, and the optional hydraulic seat. The rear PTO used a 3 GPM pump for its clutch lockup features.

The basic hydraulic system remained basically unchanged from the 56 series, except that now IH had developed its

Labeled as a Tobacco Special, this 574 was especially outfitted with a longer, extended front axle and rear wheels. Tobacco farming requires a wider-stance tractor to straddle the bedded row plants. IH captured a niche market for these tractors in the 1940s with A and B Farmall and later Cub tractors, and offered Tobacco Special tractors through the early 1980s. *State Historical Society of Wisconsin*

This photo, taken in the pasture at IH's Hickory Hills Farm, shows the new-for-1971 IH tractor lineup. Shown clockwise from the left are: 1066 w/ ROPS, 966 w/ Custom Cab, 1466 w/ Custom Cab, 574, 354, 454, and 766 Farmall tractors. IH would drop the Farmall name from its tractors in 1973. *Author Collection*

own style of rear auxiliary hydraulic couplers. The new lever-operated couplers eliminated implement hose "lockup" because you could now hook and unhook under pressure. These couplers also had a built-in breakaway protection. Ironically, IH had been using a remote hydraulic coupler on its 06-26 series that later became the industry's standard-sized coupler, adapted by the ASAE. This coupler is called the "pioneer," or ISO-style coupler. IH kept its own unique hydraulic coupler style design throughout the 66 and 86 series. Finally, only after the 50 series was announced in 1981, IH returned back to the ISO-sized coupler.

IH also improved the ease of maintenance for the hydraulic filter on the 66 series. The prior series required a gasket

to be replaced when changing the filter element. Now, on the 66 series, two wing nuts could be loosened and the cast-aluminum cover could be removed to allow access to the filter. A simple rubber O-ring was needed for filter replacement during service, not the awkward paper gasket that the previous series used.

McLaughlin Manufacturing Company of East Moline, Illinois, manufactured a totally new operator cab for IH. This was called the Deluxe Cab, and was an available option. This was another option to the previously used Custom Cab, which also remained an option. Both cabs now used heavy rubber mounting pads called ISO-MOUNTS to insulate the cab and operator from vibration and sound. IH was the pioneer in this use of

space-age technology in farm equipment and later expanded its uses to other machines during the decade.

The Deluxe two-door cab featured more than 40 square feet of tinted glass for excellent visibility in any direction. The cab was heavily upholstered for sound reduction and came with a standard heater and optional air conditioning. A choice of radios featuring AM-FM bands and eight-track tape players were optional to ease the long days of operation. A two-post ROPS with optional canopy was also available, and was replaced by a four-post ROPS with canopy in 1973.

IH tested the 1466, 966, and 1066 gear-drive and hydrostatic tractors at Nebraska in early October of 1971. The 1466 recorded 133.4 maximum PTO

horsepower, and had a 15.95 horsepower hours-per-gallon rating, which tied the previous record for fuel economy set by the 1206 in the category of 100+ PTO horsepower IH-built tractors. The IH 966 gear drive recorded 96 PTO horsepower while still delivering a 14.85 horsepower hours-per-gallon rating. The IH 1066 gear-drive model cranked out just over 116 PTO horsepower with a 15.16 horsepower hours-per-gallon rating. Only the hydrostatic-drive counterpart (1066 Hydro) produced a slightly lower PTO horsepower rating of 113.58, with a comparable fuel economy rating of 14.32.

New Color for an "Old" Tractor

In 1972, IH unveiled the "all-new" four-wheel-drive replacement for the 4156 tractor. This tractor was labeled the 4166 and was painted IH red and white, not yellow and white. It was rated at 150 horsepower and was powered by an IH-built DT-436 six-cylinder diesel with a governed engine speed of 2,400 rpm.

The 4166 was still similar to the 4156. The engine had been changed along with the paint color, but the basic cab, frame, hood, grille, and transmission were all carried over from the 4156. The 4166 still gave the operator a choice of two steering modes: front-wheel-only and four-wheel coordinated steering, either of which could be shifted into simply by moving a side-console–mounted lever. The 4166 had a 13 1/2-foot turning radius when in four-wheel steer. This was a tighter circle than most two-wheel drives could do.

A simple high-low range transmission that offered four speeds in each range (including reverse) featured a

An IH 1066 paired with an IH 650 forage harvester makes the ideal silage-making team on the farm. Because of the variable speed feature of the hydro, if a slug were incurred, the operator could slow down while maintaining full-engine PTO horsepower. This was an exclusive feature that only hydrostatic drives had. *State Historical Society of Wisconsin*

straight-line shifting pattern. (The shifting layout remained unchanged from the 4156.) Hydraulic-powered four-wheel brakes were also standard equipment, and were easily able to stop this 15,000-pound tractor.

Optional equipment that made this model the ideal small four-wheel drive included: a deluxe operator's cab with a heater and air conditioner, a field lighting package, rear 1,000-rpm PTO, a hydraulically adjustable drawbar, and a rear three-point hitch, along with a wide array of tire and weighting options.

The list price of $30,400 made the 4166 an affordable alternative to the "large" four-wheel drives, which listed for nearly $20,000 more. The 4166 production numbers were stable, with 2,565 units manufactured in its 1972–1976 production run.

Building Legendary Engines: The IH 400 Series Diesels

The 400 series of IH diesel engines proved to be a huge sales success for IH in both the ag and truck markets. IH engineers designed the 400 series, and its little brother the 300 series, to be rugged, durable power plants with tremendous torque rise and lugging ability. They provided the ultimate in serviceability and economy, they operated quietly, and they had a long life. Engineers also designed parts commonality into these engines to keep the cost of service parts low. The 400 series comprised two models, the 414- and 436-ci displacement engines. Either engine could be turbocharged or naturally aspirated. The 300 series came in two sizes, the 312 and 360.

The 400 series of engines was the culmination of over five years of engineering and research, and more than 100,000 hours of intensive development testing aimed at building a quieter-operating line of engines that could also deliver higher, steady torque rise under load. IH needed a $25 million automated tooling and equipment investment at its factory in Melrose Park, Illinois, to produce this new engine line. All these engines are inline, six-cylinder, heavy-duty diesel design.

IH's new 966 hydrostatic drive is seen here with a mounted four-bottom moldboard plow. The infinitely variable speed control of the hydrostatic-drive transmission meant the operator could slow down or speed up with full engine power to get jobs done faster and without clutching or changing gears.
Author Collection

The Big Red of the new IH 66 series was the model 1466. Using an IH-built six-cylinder turbocharged diesel engine with a displacement of 436 ci, the 1466 was for operators who needed big "red power" on their farms. The 1466 were a popular model for IH, with over 25,000 tractors being made during its 1971 to 1976 production. *State Historical Society of Wisconsin*

To help keep tooling costs down and ensure rapid parts availability, IH engineers designed the 400 series engines with a 90 percent parts interchangeability between the two basic displacements. IH also put many new features into this engine series, among them heavier main bearings and Elotherm-hardened crankshafts that increased fatigue strength up to 80 percent. A new process of sleeve honing called plateau honing was used to provide a smoother surface for better oil retention and longer engine life. A totally new full-pressure engine lubrication system continuously circulated 100 percent filtered oil. It was driven by a crankshaft-mounted Gerotor-style pump to lubricate bearings, turbo, timing gears, and piston cooling jets. Dual spin-on full-flow filters and a large, externally mounted oil cooler kept engine oil clean and cool.

The cooling system was designed to eliminate engine hot spots by splitting the coolant flow to both the engine oil cooler and the cylinder water jacket. This high-flow cooling system allowed maximum "scrubbing" around the sleeves for better heat exchange and it worked well, except for one Achilles heel called cavitation erosion. By the 86 series, however, IH finally found a cure for this.

"I Want to Have a V-8!"

This was the quote that an IH executive allegedly made after hearing that Massey-Ferguson had in development a V-8–powered row-crop tractor called model 1155. To compete with this, IH decided to use the naturally aspirated model DV-550 V-8 diesel from its truck division for the power plant. The DV-550 had an eight-cylinder bore in block (no sleeves) design. Two prototype models were built: models 1068 and 1468. The 1068 used a DV-550 engine coupled to a 1066 drivetrain. The 1468 was identical, except that it used the drivetrain from a 1466. After thorough field testing, the 1468 was selected to be the production model. The 68 series was unique among IH tractors because its dual exhaust stacks made the tractor look like a hot rod.

The DV-550 engine had a feature never seen before in a farm tractor: At an idle, and under light loads, the V-8 engine operated on only four cylinders

Small enough for large farms and large enough for small farms was the model 766. Offered in either gasoline- or diesel-powered versions, the 766 was suited for any task. The tractor having a ROPS and canopy along with front ballast weights made cultivating this field of soybeans an enjoyable task. The 766 replaced the popular model 756 in 1971. *State Historical Society of Wisconsin*

(1-4-6-7). This offered exceptional fuel economy under light loads. When the engine needed more power, the governor in the injection pump activated the other four cylinders. Some people thought the 68 series sounded strange when running on only four, but it was normal. Many farmers had this feature on their 68 series bypassed and had the engine running on eight all the time.

The 1468 V-8 was the last tractor tested at the Nebraska Tractor Test Lab in 1972. Testing started on November 9 and ended on December 7. While at Nebraska, the 1468 recorded an output of 145.49 maximum PTO horsepower. The 1468 developed a 15.6 horsepower hours-per-gallon fuel economy rating at maximum output. This rating was nearly identical to the Massey 1155 V8, the competition's direct comparison model. The 1468 sold well, with 2,905 tractors manufactured during its 1971–1974 production run—not bad for a fill-in model.

Many of the aftermarket "will fitters" decided the easiest way to get more power from any tractor was to add a turbocharger. The V-8 engine allowed the use of twin turbochargers to generate more horsepower. This may have been a good short-term choice, but the DV-550 engine was not designed to absorb the stresses that a turbo creates. Consequently, many 68 series V-8s suffered a premature death because of this, usually by ejecting a connecting rod through the side of the block.

New Horsepower Ratings for the 66 Series

In 1973, IH increased the engine horsepower on the 966, 1066, and 1466 tractors by increasing the rated engine speed from 2,400 rpm to 2,600 rpm. This was done to keep the IH 66 series models a step ahead in horsepower rating of both the newly released Generation II John Deere 30 series and the 7000 series Allis-Chalmers tractors. IH was required to have these new "high horsepower" 66 series tractors retested at the Nebraska Tractor Test Lab, which was done in late April through early May of 1973. The first of the beefed-up 66 series tractors to be tested was the model 966 gear drive, which jumped to a 100.8 PTO horsepower rating—an increase of 4 horsepower. The fuel economy rating, however, dropped to 14.54 horsepower hours-per-gallon of fuel. The 1066 fared much the same, reaching a horsepower rating of 125.68, but decreasing its fuel economy rating to 14.93. The 1466 now became the IH row-crop tractor horsepower leader, with a rating of 145.85 PTO horsepower.

IH also stopped selling the Custom Cab on the 66 series tractors in 1973. Instead, the IH-built two-door Deluxe Cab was restyled with a new two-tone red/white paint scheme, replacing the previously all-white painted cab. The cab interior was changed to red, with only a white painted roof. A wider lip was installed on the doorsill to retain the deeply padded floor mat better. The lower window in the cab doors was eliminated, and engineers enlarged the side cab windows and increased their opening radius to 30 degrees. They also put on a new door handle with a key lock, and replaced the inside door latch lever to provide easier entry and exit for the operator.

Another change on the 66 series was a wider lower rear window, which provided an even more expansive view of the hitch and PTO. The opening rear window now tilted out 26 inches, or a whopping 67 degrees, compared to the old cab window, which only opened 18.5 inches, or 48 degrees. This greatly reduced the operator's reach for levers on choppers or other pull-type equipment. A large ashtray was also added to the right-hand side of the cab, beside the operator's seat. Finally, optional AM, AM-FM, or eight-track stereo radio

The 1566 model offered as optional equipment an all-new IH-built two-door operator cab. This cab had an integral ROPS frame to protect the operator in case of a tractor.upset. Large tinted glass windows gave the operator outstanding visibility in any direction. Air conditioning, AM-FM radio, and eight-track tape player were but a few of the options offered on this cab.
State Historical Society of Wisconsin

inserts were now prewired for simple installation. Clearly, the 1974 cab redesign was not just a "Du Pont paint" overhaul.

A four-post ROPS replaced the previous two-post design. The reasoning was that as tractors got bigger and heavier, a two-post ROPS was not sufficient to protect the operator in case of a tractor rollover.

The First with 5 Million Tractors

It had been nearly 10 years—1964—since International Harvester had built tractor number 4 million; now it was time to build the 5 millionth. In 1973 the company formed a committee to determine the best method of calling public attention to the appearance of IH's 5 millionth tractor. One of the committee's suggestions was to build one commemorative 1066 for each dealer, which would require the manufacture of an estimated 3,000 units. The management at IH could pretty easily determine when the 5 millionth was going to be made, but it needed an adequate lead time to do the required preliminary work.

The initial specifications of the 5 millionth would be those of a standard 1066 Farmall tractor with Deluxe Cab, two hydraulic valves, hitch, and the model's standard equipment. IH estimated that the special effects added to the basic 1066 would add about $300 to its base price. The specs IH had in mind for the 1066s were as follows:

• Chrome-plate the grille, grille shroud, nameplates and hub caps, muffler, front and rear wheels, keys, control levers, and fuel and radiator caps

The IH tractor lineup for 1973 included (clockwise from upper left) 454, 1066 Turbo, 966, 454, 966 Hydro, 1066 Hydro, 1466, 354, and 766. Wide front ends were now the norm for tractors, but IH still offered narrow front ends if the farmer needed it. The use of ROPS devices was made mandatory by OSHA as tractors grew bigger and more powerful. *Author Collection*

"Ask the neighbor about his new IH 1066 hydro, he'll tell ya." That's exactly what the new 66 series hydrostatic drives were causing, a lot of talk among neighbors. And why not, the smooth, clutchless, single lever design of the hydro made it a favorite among thousands of IH customers. *Author Collection*

- Include a special nameplate indicating the 5 millionth tractor
- Install a special nameplate inscribed with the name of the customer that purchases the tractor
- Install special floor mat and cab upholstery, use a special colored covering on the seat and give a special effect to the steering wheel and cap by using a colored wheel or clear wheel with red flecks in the plastic

After IH marketing had listed its "dream specs" for the 5 millionth, the promotional department listed its ideas for the 1066. Committee members suggested:

1. Develop a special semi-tractor foldout trailer with steps for quick setup, carrying a restored Farmall tractor along with the 5 millionth 1066. The trailer would be equipped with sound and Super 8 film showing the history of IH tractors. This would be taken to every major farm show in the country for publicity.

2. Cover various cutaway areas with Plexiglas so the public could see the important features with appropriate signage. Chrome the interior displayed parts.

3. Even if the unit were not displayed as suggested in the previous two ideas, it should still be hauled to the various farm shows for display.

To dispose of the unit, IH suggested doing the following:

1. Give it to the Smithsonian Institution or other historical society for display

2. Develop a national contest in which individuals buying a new Farmall between certain dates would have the chance to win it

3. Give it to the Future Farmers of America or YFA

4. Put it on display at the Living History Farm near Des Moines, Iowa, alongside other older tractors, with ownership remaining with IH

5. Build a special display for it at the Museum of Science and Industry in Chicago, Illinois.

Finally, after rationalizing the costs and manufacturing logistics of building 3,000 special tractors, IH decided to build only one IH 5 millionth. This

One lever speed control meant slugs were a thing of the past with the new IH 966 hydrostatic-drive tractor. Using a D-414 IH-built six-cylinder naturally aspirated engine the 966 was the ideal PTO operation tractor. By moving the S-R lever, the driver could vary travel speed while maintaining full engine PTO horsepower to the chopper. *Author Collection*

time, however, instead of just slapping a decal or sign on the side of a tractor (as it had done with the other IH millionth tractors), IH decided to go all out and do a fully customized version, similar to the earlier proposed units.

The actual 1066 used to build the 5 millionth IH tractor was SN #35153, and it was finally assembled during the week of January 6, 1974, and shipped to Hinsdale on or about January 10 for its modifications. Later in January, the 1066 was returned to Farmall for its unveiling.

On February 1, 1974, after the 9 a.m. factory break time, IH rolled out its 5 millionth tractor, a specially painted 1066 Farmall turbo diesel tractor with cab. It featured a hand-applied paint design along with some special pinstriping. IH decided to have the muffler, grille, and front wheels chromed to add some flash. The cab's interior remained stock in appearance, unlike the earlier suggested custom upholstery idea.

The first public showing of the 1066 5 millionth was at the 1974 National Farm Machinery Show held annually in Louisville, Kentucky. Here it drew the farmers' attention, and many asked if they could buy a 1066 painted like the 5 millionth. IH executives had considered building a limited run of real "replica" 5 millionths to sell, but it was eventually decided to make one tractor and do some special types of promotions with it. At every show that the tractor appeared, IH would hand out certificates stating that you had seen the 5 millionth IH tractor on display at the show. Today these certificates can be very rare and valuable to the collector.

The IH dealer network also benefited from the 5 millionth tractor release. Each dealer received a special limited edition (one per dealer) full-color poster. The poster had an artist's drawing of both the 5 millionth and one of the first

tractors made in 1906 above a color photo of the 5 millionth. The poster simply stated across the top "5 Millionth 1906–1974. Few of these posters survive today. Those that do are quite rare and worth several hundred dollars to the avid IH collector.

In an advertising department memo dated January 10, 1974, IH execs developed several ideas on how to promote the 5 millionth tractor, some of which were actually used and others not. Among the suggested ideas for promotions were:

- Playing cards or specially embossed drinking mugs to be used for dealer promotional use
- Commemorative paperweights with the 5 millionth tractor photo encased in plastic
- Overseas publicity and advertising promotion
- Creation of a commemorative scale-model toy replica of the 5 millionth

Sporting a new red-and-white paint scheme, the 4166 four-wheel drive was painted to match the rest of the ag tractor lineup. The engine on the 4166 was now a DT-436 that developed over 150 PTO horsepower—that's 10 horsepower more than the 4156 it replaced. IH built just over 2,500 of the 4166 during its 1972 to 1976 production period. *Author Collection*

- Photos and press releases of the 5 millionth leaving the assembly line
- Building a commemorative toy replica using an ERTL 1066 toy.

IH seriously considered building a toy replica to sell through its dealers, but the idea was rejected as too expensive. A farm toy collector named Rick Campbell (who saw the real 5 millionth on display at the Minnesota State Fair) decided he wanted a toy model of this tractor, so he built one using an ERTL 1066 toy body. Many other toy collectors (including this author) saw the craftsmanship of his work and had Rick build one just like his original. In 1991 the ERTL Company was planning to re-release the IH 66 series toy tractors in a slightly modified form from the original issue. One of the

Campbell 5 millionths was sent to ERTL and the "official" 5 millionth toy was finally made, even if it was over 15 years late and not an "exact replica." A few years later, ERTL made the 1/64 scale version of the 5 millionth IH tractor.

At the dealer introductory meeting for the new IH 86 series Pro Ag line of tractors (held in Chicago, Illinois, September 26, 1976), IH decided to auction off the 5 millionth tractor to the highest bidder. Any IH dealer could bid on the 1066. Of the 177 bids entered, a group of 13 dealers from Montana submitted the winning bid. IH sold the 5 millionth tractor to the Montana dealer group for $40,086.86, then donated the proceeds of the sale to a research project, which Montana State University would administer.

A specially cast plaque was affixed to the front of the tractor that listed the 13 IH dealers who purchased the 5 millionth. Along with this was a story of the 5 millionth. It read:

"When this tractor was produced at International Harvester's Farmall Plant in Rock Island, Illinois, IH became the first manufacturer to claim the production of 5 million tractors.

"The following two years it was featured at fairs, conventions and shows across the United States.

"On September 26, 1976, it was offered to all IH dealers attending a new 86 series tractor announcement in Chicago.

"The keys to this tractor were presented to these dealers on November 5, 1976, at their convention in Great

Falls, Montana. It was immediately announced that the proceeds of this auction would be used to establish a research program under the direction of Montana State University for a study to further improve tractor operating efficiencies."

The 5 millionth was hauled to Montana in March of 1977. Once there, it spent nearly the next two decades being shuffled from one of the winning-bid dealers to another for their open houses or other events. After nearly 23 years of being moved from one dealer to another, the 5 millionth finally found a permanent home in 1997. It now is on display at the Montana State Ag Museum in Conrad, Montana.

IH Four-Wheel Drives Meet the Tractor Horsepower Race

When IH introduced its model 4300 four-wheel drive in 1960, it set upon a course that would change the way farm tractor design would be for the rest of the century. After the Frank Hough Industrial Division of IH had built several four-wheel-drive models, it became apparent that a change was needed. For IH to engineer and tool up for an entirely new four-wheel-drive tractor line would be cost prohibitive. But there was an alternative.

Instead, IH turned to an outside vendor to have one of its tractors rebadged as an IH product. In the fall of 1970, IH began a joint venture with a company called Mississippi Road Supply (MRS). IH had supplied MRS with W9s, WD9s, and other IH tractors for modification into various types of powered earth-moving equipment since the 1940s. The joint venture would use IH's engineering and testing expertise, financial stability, and dealer marketing organization to sell the tractors MRS would build.

MRS built for IH two articulated models of 155 and 130 horsepower each and was scheduled to take over the production of the current 4156. The joint venture was to license the three current MRS models (which even included a 236 PTO horsepower model) into new models for IH. MRS would

This rear-corner view of the 4166 shows the working end of the tractor. A wide swinging drawbar and rear-mounted fuel tank were standard equipment. The three-point hitch and rear PTO attachments were optional. The large box at the rear of the operator's cab housed a filter to clean the air entering the cab. *Author Collection*

now use IH's DT-466 and DV-550 engines for the tractors, and IH would provide the marketing and distribution.

The management at IH agreed to a three-year contract to sell the MRS's rebadged tractors. The MRS model A-60 was now labeled as the IH 4166, the A-75 was the 4168, the A-80 was the IH 4266, the A-100 (still retaining its 6-71 Detroit Diesel engine) was the 4366, and production of the A-105 (also Detroit powered) was slated to begin in February of 1971 to become the new IH 4468, with a dealer announcement scheduled for June of 1971. For reasons still unknown, the joint venture dissolved quickly and IH began shopping for a new four-wheel-drive tractor vendor. It found one in Fargo, North Dakota. The name of this company was Steiger.

IH bought a 28 percent share of the newly incorporated Steiger Tractor Co. and quickly set out to bring tractors to

the market and make up lost time from the ill-fated MRS venture. IH proposed using its own engines in Steiger-built chassis (just like the MRS venture). It was a good deal for both companies. IH gained a well-built tractor and Steiger received some much-needed cash and tractor orders to keep its expanding business growing. Only one of the proposed models from the MRS venture was built by Steiger (the 4366); the rest were not.

The 4366 was part Steiger, part IH, combining a Steiger-built cab and front and rear frames with an IH engine and final drive assemblies from a 1466. The 4366 used a Fuller five-speed constant-mesh transmission with a hi-low section providing 10 forward and 2 reverse speeds. Use of the 1466 final drives for the drive axle was ingenious. The rear axle was a stock production unit with the differential lock and brakes

This furrow shot shows the big-power IH 4166 pulling an eight-bottom IH 700 plow. The choice of four- or two-wheel steering on the 4166 made plowing straight furrows easy, even in irregularly shaped fields. The 4166 shown here has the new-for-1974 red-painted cab. IH switched to red-painted cabs with white-painted roofs in 1974. *Author Collection*

deleted. The front axle was another 1466 final drive with the ring and pinion reversed for forward operation. Both axles were pressure lubed and cooled. The use of 118-inch bar-type axles allowed the choice of either large single- or dual-drive wheels. To keep the drive shafts from "chattering," the 4366 used a "swinging" transfer case. This gear case moved in the same direction as the tractor was turning to lessen the wear on universal joints and driveline angles.

The front and rear frames could oscillate to keep all four wheels in contact with the ground. The articulated steering was easy to operate as it was fully hydrostatic. A 17-gallon-per-minute tandem hydraulic pump made the 4366 easy to turn at low engine rpms. A 40-degree articulation allowed a 15-foot turning radius (with 78-inch wheel tread). This was shorter than even many two-wheel drives could do.

The two-door cab was basically the Steiger "Safari" cab painted IH 935 white. In 1974 the cab was changed, to be painted IH red with a white roof only. The instrument panel featured an engine tachometer/speedometer, engine oil pressure, fuel level, and air filter restriction gauges. The floor-mounted shifter, along with the console-mounted clutch and brake pedals, gave a clean open floor for the operator. Rubber Isomounts on the cab mounting

Disking corn stubble was easy work for this 4166 when it's teamed with an IH tandem disk harrow. The big DT436 engine and planetary hub-style final drives deliver power to the ground for more work done and less slippage. The front-mounted ballast weights aid in the tractor's traction and weight balance. *State Historical Society of Wisconsin*

points helped keep vibration away from the operator for an even smoother, quieter ride. A heavy rubber floor mat and other cab insulation also kept engine noise and heat away from the operator. Fresh, clean-filtered air was brought to the dual blower-pressurizing fan. A choice of radio options, along with optional air conditioning, added year-round operating enjoyment. After a hard day's farming with a 4366, the operator would still be comfortable, thanks to the amenities of the cab.

A large 141-gallon fuel tank was an integral part of the rear frame. This put working weight where it was needed: on the rear drive axle. The 4366 had a 2/3-1/3 weight balance: 2/3 of the tractor's weight was on the front axle, and 1/3 on the rear. As the rear axle was loaded by the implement pull, weight was "transferred" from the front to the rear, giving an ideal 50-50 weight distribution under load. An optional three-point rear hitch made the use of large mounted implements very convenient.

In 1975, IH added a V-8 diesel-powered four-wheel drive to the lineup. This was the model 4568. The 4568 used IH's model V-800 engine and was built by Steiger, too. This was a turbocharged V-8 diesel with a displacement of 800 ci. To fit the V-8 diesel, IH needed more engine cooling, so a wider frame was developed that would allow a larger radiator to be used. The 4568 used the final drive axle assembly from a 1466 for its front and rear axles. The 4568 did not offer a three-point hitch option. In 1976, when the 86 series was announced, IH relabeled the 4366 as the 4836 and the 4568 became the 4586. Both were restriped to look similar to the other 86 series.

The IH-Steiger connection proved very fruitful for both companies. IH had a 28 percent share of the four-wheel-drive market in the mid-1970s. The sales of the 4366 and 4568 helped prove it. The 4366 sold 3,166 units from 1973–1976, and the 4568 sold 857 units in its short 1975-1976 production run.

Big Power in a Little Tractor

In 1972, IH announced the new 66 horsepower replacement for its ever-popular (and finally just retired) model 656 tractor. This tractor was designated the IH 666. The 666 was offered in both gear drive (10 forward and 2 reverse speeds with optional TA and hydrostatic-drive versions. Using either an IH-built C-291 six-cylinder gasoline or D-312 six-cylinder diesel engine as its power plant, the 666 was a popular-sized tractor. Hundreds of 666s were used for lease units to large corporate farms, canning companies, and other large-scale enterprises. A number of 666s have also found their home on the farms of America doing various chores or performing as the main tractor in fieldwork.

Photographed in the back lot at IH's Hinsdale, Illinois, Engineering Test Center, this 1468 V-8 diesel tractor is pulling two IH 400 Cyclo Air planters in a new duplex hitch. The 1468 was unique in operating on only four cylinders at an idle, and then on all eight under higher rpms. The 1468 V-8 used a DV-550 engine "borrowed" from the IH truck division to compete against the Massey-Ferguson 1155 tractor. *Author Collection*

One of the most exciting days on any farm is the arrival of a new tractor. Here an IH dealer is unloading a new 1468 V-8 diesel as the anxious farm couple looks on. The 1468 had unique dual exhaust stacks that gave the tractor a hot rod look. Today 1468s are fast becoming very collectible. *State Historical Society of Wisconsin*

Many features found on the bigger 66 series were also offered on the 666. The choice of wide or narrow front ends, along with various-sized rear tires, meant the 666 could be tailored to fit any farming operation. Fully hydrostatic power steering along with cowl-mounted shifting controls (like the bigger 66s had) meant easy operation. A deluxe padded six-way adjustable seat with suspension helped smooth out the ride over rough fields. Also, the operator's platform and fenders had rubber ISOMOUNT mounts

to reduce vibration, leaving the operator feeling fresh after a long day's work.

A host of optional equipment was also available on the 666: An electric air cleaner restriction gauge told you when the engine's air filter needed service. An optional fender-mounted AM-FM radio could be added, as could a two-post ROPS and sunshade canopy.

A power-shift 540-rpm-only PTO allowed you to feather the load for smooth even PTO operation. The rear-mounted hydraulic couplers could be

coupled under pressure. There was a choice of either a two-point Fast Hitch or category II three-point hitch with swinging drawbar. The 666 could also be ordered in a high-clearance version.

The 666 used basically the same transmission and final drive as the popular-selling 656, but the hood and grille were restyled to reflect the 66 series tractor family appearance. During the 1972–1976 production run of the 666, a total of 9,367 tractors were made. When the 86 series was introduced in

On February 1, 1974, at 9 A.M., IH rolled its 5 millionth tractor off the assembly line at the Farmall Plant in Rock Island, Illinois. IH was the first tractor manufacturer to produce 5 million tractors. Here Mr. McAllister is seen driving the 1066 5 millionth that day to the cheers of the crowd. Today the 1066 5 millionth is safely stored in a museum in Montana. *State Historical Society of Wisconsin*

1976, the model 666 was restriped to become the model 686. In 1979, the D-312 diesel engine in the 686 was replaced with the Neuss-built IH D-310 "German diesel" engine. Later that year, the 686 was dropped from the IH tractor line.

The Race for Big Horsepower

IH was locked in an ever-increasing horsepower race with Deere, A-C, Case, Ford, and Massey in the early 1970s. It seemed that the bigger the horsepower, the bigger the sales volume. IH decided to look into another way of delivering more horsepower to the ground.

The current transmission/final drive design was nearly maxed out for horsepower reserve, so IH designed a new unitized powertrain with a planetary final drive, a high-low range, and a three-speed transmission gearbox. Two models were developed from this new drivetrain. IH engineers believed this new modular design would be the answer for higher horsepower tractor design of the future, and they were partially right. The inboard-mounted wet-type multidisc brakes could handle the added horsepower, but servicing them was much more difficult than the old bull-gear drive style. A hydraulically assisted clutch reduced pedal efforts considerably.

Testing of this new "component" style transmission began in earnest during 1971. A prototype unit designated TX 96 II was photographed on a bright October 17, 1971 in the back lot of the Hinsdale Engineering Center. TX 96 II was sporting the all-new IH-designed planetary final drive transmission assembly. A single-speed (1,000 rpm only) PTO, dual remote hydraulic

Immediately after the ceremonies at Farmall, the 1066 5 millionth hit the road for several public appearances, the first one being the National Farm Machinery Show in Louisville, Kentucky. Here, in this rare color shot of the 5 millionth at Louisville, you can see that its unique paint scheme and chrome trim really do create a stir and have everyone talking. *State Historical Society of Wisconsin*

IH's entry into the large articulated four-wheel-drive market came with the new model 4366 four-wheel drive. The 4366 was created Using an IH-built DT-466 engine and IH final drives and styling, along with a Steiger-built frame, cab, and transmission. The 164-horsepower 4366 needed to use dual wheels all around for flotation and traction. This would be the first of several models that were jointly made by Steiger for IH. *Author Collection*

valves, and a three-point hitch were all fitted to the rear of the tractor. This tractor was later labeled the IH 1568 V-8 diesel tractor.

The two tractor models using this new component-style drivetrain were a 160-horsepower 1566, powered by a six-cylinder, inline design, turbocharged DT-436 IH-built diesel engine, and a 160-horsepower model 1568. The 1568 was similar to the 1566, but was powered by an IH-built DV-550 naturally aspirated V-8 engine instead. When the 1568 model was released for production, the 1468 V-8 was dropped.

The DV-550 engine in the 1568 was an improved version over the 1468. It had higher compression pistons, higher-pressure injection nozzles (2,800 psi opening pressure versus 2,300 psi on the 1468), a new injection pump that used cylinders 2-3-5-8 for idling, and new cylinder heads with increased valve recession (to prevent valve to piston interference). IH Service Bulletin #S-2944 listed these improvements for the DV-550 engine and stated that from then on, IH would only service the newer 1975 model engine parts. If an older 1468 needed new pistons, only the new 1975 version pistons would be offered. These new-style pistons were not to be inter-mixed with the older-style pistons in an engine. If the old cylinder head was to be reused, the valves had to be reground to have additional recession on both the intake and exhaust.

Both models of the 1500 series were available with a choice of options such as four-post ROPS, IH deluxe cab, air conditioning, tilting steering wheel, dual rear wheels, FWA, and other options.

Introduced in 1975, the IH 4568 was the big brother to the 4366. The 4568 used an IH-built DVT-800 engine as its power plant. This V-8 had an 800-ci displacement and was also turbocharged. IH needed a larger four-wheel drive as demand for big implements grew. The 4568 used larger final drives than the 4366 had and were built in 1975 and 1976. The model 4586 replaced it in 1976. *Author Collection*

Moving from a farm field was quick working with the IH 666 diesel. The 10 forward and 2 reverse speeds (when equipped with TA) gave the operator a wide selection of speeds. This 66 is outfitted with a two-post ROPS and canopy for operator protection. *Author Collection*

However, as with nearly all of the "high horsepower" IH tractors made, only a single speed 1,000 rpm-only PTO unit was offered as optional equipment on each model. The 1566 and 1568 were produced exclusively in 1975 and 1976, with the 1566 production numbers running to 7,417 units and the 1568 to 862 units.

Relabel an Old Tractor into a New One

Since it had marketed hydrostatic-drive tractors, IH had been experiencing a lot of criticism due to its method of labeling these tractors. After all, a 1066 hydro should have been as good

as a 1066 gear drive, but that turned out not to be true. A 1066 hydro only delivered the drawbar horsepower of a 966 gear drive. This was due to the parasitic losses and inefficiencies that were found in hydrostatic-drive tractors—and it was causing IH to lose sales.

To combat this, IH relabeled the 966 Hydro and 1066 Hydro as the new Hydro 100. The Hydro 100 used a D-436 naturally aspirated six-cylinder diesel engine. IH also relabeled the 666 Hydro as the Hydro 70. A new white striping over the hood side was the main identifying mark of this "new" hydro. The production of these two models, which ran from 1973 to 1976,

totaled 5,431 units for the Hydro 100 and 3,022 for the Hydro 70.

The Hydros were not the only tractors IH would relabel; the entire 66 series of row-crop tractors was restriped for 1976 and marketed as the "Black Stripe" 66 series. The new paint scheme changed the old white-painted side panels to IH red, and a black stripe with white pinstripe border was introduced, along with white numbers and letters. The black stripe started at the rear of the hood cowling and moved toward the front, making an abrupt turn up and over the hood's side and top. This gave the 66 series a fresh new look, and helped keep IH sales going too. The boom years of 1973 and

1974, when tractors couldn't be made fast enough, were followed by slower production in 1975 and 1976. The 66 series sold well, as evidenced by their strong production numbers: 10,799 units for the 766; 21,017 for the 966; a staggering 54,947 for the 1066; and 25,264 units for the 1466.

The careful IH observer would note that when the stripe changed or a special paint job was added, it was time for IH to retire the series, and this proved the case with the 66 series too. The stripe color change was only a prelude to the next change IH had planned for the farmer, representing a new level of power and comfort never seen before from IH: the new IH 86 series Pro Ag line of tractors.

The IH Pro Ag Line: The IH 86 Series

In September of 1976, IH invited all of its ag dealers to its Chicago headquarters for the unveiling of the IH 86 series Pro Ag line. This was a totally new look in farming: A new tractor series built with the operator's comfort in mind and built for the professional agri-businessman.

The new IH 86 series tractors comprised six basic models. The 85-horsepower 886, 100-horsepower 986, 125-horsepower 1086, 145-horsepower 1486, 161-horsepower 1586, and the 100-horsepower hydrostatic-drive 186 Hydro. IH also restriped the 666 and Hydro 70 models and renamed them the 686 and Hydro 86, respectively. The 986, 1086, and 186 Hydro were also sold as high-clearance models.

The new IH 86 series still retained the same basic grille, hoods, engine, and drivetrain that had been used in the previous 66 series, but it featured a totally new operator cab called the Control Center. This cab offered space age design in a modern farm tractor. IH had added a few drivetrain improvements, most notably self-adjusting, wet hydraulic-powered brakes. All of the 86 series tractors had outboard-mounted wet multidisc-type brakes (except the 1586s, which were internal) for easy service. A switch mounted on the brake housing even alerted the operator when the brakes were worn or needed service. The muffler was located under the hood, allowing a nearly unobstructed front view. The only drawbacks to this were higher engine-compartment and sometimes cab-floor temperatures. A muffler eliminator was offered by an aftermarket manufacturer to lower the exhaust back pressure and open up the engine area. The TA was also improved. The sprags were 20 percent wider than previous models, the tractor had positive clutch engagement, 30 percent more bearing load capacity, and 50 percent more increase in general capacity. The TA was controlled via cable instead of mechanical linkage. The optional PTO on the 1586 now had a hydraulically operated brake.

The major difference between the IH 86 series Pro Ag line and the 66 series was the operator's cab. (The 86 series adapted the cab from the XCF-65 tractor that IH had planned to use as the 66 series replacement. Cost of production restraints and other financial issues killed the project, however, and only the cab was salvaged.) With this totally new cab, the operator still had two doors for easy entry and exit to either side. The total glass area increased to 43.2 square feet, with scoop-type opening side windows and a larger opening rear window. The new cab featured a built-in protective frame exceeding SAE and OSHA standards. But perhaps its major feature was that now the operator sat 1.5 feet farther forward than in past machines, for a smoother operator's ride and easier entry and exit. The two double-wall construction automotive-type doors had heavy rubber seals on them to keep dirt out and improve operator comfort. A rear-mounted cab air filter self-cleaned every time the doors were shut, and IH added a three-speed cab ventilation fan for even greater comfort. With this model, IH engineers had made the tractor's air-conditioning system "smart" by adding an au-

In this photo dated October 14, 1971, the tractor model QFE-7881 (more commonly known as the model 1568 V-8) was photographed in the back lot at IH's Hinsdale, Illinois, Engineering Center. Even though the tractor has "Turbo" decals on the hood, the engine is still naturally aspirated. The 1568 was released for production in 1975, using a new modular designed transmission with an inboard planetary final drive. *State Historical Society of Wisconsin*

tomatic monitor and shutdown system, which would shut the A-C system down before damage could occur to its components. A red warning light in the cab illuminated when the system was activated.

Optional equipment included a choice of AM-FM-CB radios and tape players and a hydraulic suspended seat. A cloth-covered seat became available after 1978.

IH used two 12-volt maintenance-free sealed batteries in the 86 series. These batteries seem to be super power cells, as even a few 86 series models being used today still have the original factory-installed batteries in them. A rugged Delco starter and alternator were also standard equipment.

The use of electronics had reached the farm when IH offered its initially optional

(except on the Hydro 186, then later standard for all models) digital data center module in the 86 series. This dash-mounted control box gave the operator instant digital readouts of the engine rpm, power takeoff rpm, exhaust gas temperature, and travel speed. The 86 series also used modular, plug-in-type instrument cluster gauges for fuel, voltmeter, engine oil pressure, and engine temperature.

Nothing beats the pride in owning the best. And owning a new IH 1566 turbo diesel is one of the best moves a farmer could make. Rated at 161 PTO horsepower, the 1566 was for the farmer who needed raw power in a row-crop tractor. In this photo, the whole family is excited about the 1566's arrival at the farm. *Author Collection*

The large capacity fuel tank was mounted behind the control center. An auxiliary side-mounted fuel tank increased total capacity to 85 gallons, which allowed the operator to work all day and most of the night with stopping for fuel. This was a feature that could be critical at planting or harvest time.

All the IH 86 series were sold with a two-year 1,500 hour-of-use warranty, which was something unheard of at the time. Even today, some of the competition doesn't offer this.

Almost immediately after the release of the 86 series, service bulletins announcing tractor improvements were landing in dealership mailboxes. Not all of them were bad news, in fact many were to alert you to new upgrades the factory had done and that could be added to your customers' machines when they needed repair. One of the first improvements was to the 1086 and 1486 differential lock clutches. Both had the plate and disc numbers increased for longer reliability.

In March of 1977, IH announced that the front windshield opening in the Control Center Cabs had been discovered to be too large, and the glass had fit too loosely. To keep the early production run of tractors progressing, IH added a filler strip of metal to the cab. The height of the glass was increased by 7.6 mm, and a new rubber seal was introduced to help retain the glass better. In April 1977, after numerous customer complaints, IH announced the addition of a second pocket to the cab doors, allowing easier entry and exit from the cab. IH also offered a chrome door rail handle set that could be installed by the owner. Hundreds of these rail sets were sold and are still available today.

Another assembly line shot showing (L to R) a 766, Hydro 100, and a 1066 Turbo Diesel. A Deluxe IH operator's cab hangs from the chain hoist awaiting installation on a tractor, as does the FWA axle on the shop cart below it. IH offered FWA as a factory-installed option on the 806 and 706 in 1964. *Author Collection*

IH's replacement for the 666 Hydro was the restriped Hydro 70 tractor. While basically the same as the 666, the Hydro 70 shared the same over-the-hood stripe its big brother the Hydro 100 had. IH condensed its lineup of hydro tractors in 1974 to eliminate confusion between the gear-drive and hydro-drive horsepower differences of the same model. *Author Collection*

In 1978, IH seemed to give the 86s a "tune-up." First, in February, a new lighter park lock spring was used to allow easier removal of the tractor from park gear. August brought two more improvements; a switch was added to the RANGE shift lever to allow starting the tractor when it was in park without depressing the clutch pedal. The cab steps were also changed. The narrow ladder rung style that IH had originally used was replaced by a wide-tread platform that was less likely to cause feet to slip. The 88 series 2+2 alone still retained the narrow steps, or tire interference would occur.

With the release of the B series engines in 1979, IH could now recommend the use of a 200-hour engine oil change interval (if IH oil was being used). This not only cut the owner's maintenance expense, but also conserved oil use.

IH made relatively few changes to the 86 in 1979 and 1980 prior to the Power Priority Hydraulics (PPH) series. A major internal change IH did make was to change the countershaft in the speed transmission to left-hand threads. On occasion, if the stake washer tab was not

Nebrasksa Tractor Tests: 1973-1981			
Model	**Engine**	**Test No.**	**PTO Power**
786	D-358 Diesel	1388	80
886	D-360 Diesel	1254	86
886	D-358 Diesel	1339	100
986	D-436 Diesel	1255	105
1086	DT-414 Diesel	1247	131
1486	DT-414 Diesel	1125	145
1586	DT-436 Diesel	1248	161
186 Hydro	D-436 Diesel	1257	105

IH gave the 66 series tractors a cosmetic tune-up in 1976. The white-painted side panels were now red, and a long black stripe followed the hood line and extended up over its front. These were commonly called the "Black Stripe" 66 series. The "Black Stripe" tractors were only made in 1976 and had some of the new features the forthcoming 86 series would also include. Many of the IH 66 series tractors being repainted today are done as "Black Stripe" models. *Author Collection*

bent over, the nut would unscrew and gear binding would occur. A water filter was also added to all 886s built after SN#14472 (1-16-79).

Finally, IH fixed a serious problem that had been a thorn since the 86 series release, the SMV. Originally, IH had an adhesive-backed SMV decal emblem stuck to the plastic rear fuel tank. If the tank were overfilled, spilled fuel would weaken and eventually destroy the decal adhesive. At first IH recommended cleaning the area, and then reapplying a new SMV. Later a service bulletin was issued to announce a metal bracket was available for field installation. In a later service bulletin, IH announced the availability of a new rear fuel tank with holes in it that would accept special plastic bolts to hold a metal SMV sign. Problem and safety issues solved.

IH made a few rare variations on the 86 series. In 1979 the company produced a run of 1086 and 1486 tractors with Bosch inline fuel injection pumps. These tractors were somewhat harder to start, but they had tremendous torque rise—greater even than the "normal" Ambac injection pump-equipped 86 series had had. In 1978, IH built a test lot (483 units) of 1486 tractors equipped with Schwitzer-brand turbochargers, replacing the standard issue Air Research turbo.

The main competition to the IH 86 series came from John Deere. In the fall of 1977, Deere introduced its "newest" tractor series, the 40 series. John Deere called this series the "Iron Horses," and claimed they had more iron and more horsepower than the previous 30 series of Deeres did. Basically, however, they were the old 30 series warmed over again. Deere marketing was clever in leading farmers to believe the 40 series would be much more reliable for them than the 30 had been. Back in 1960, when Deere went to six-cylinder engines in its tractors, its marketing theme was "use a lightweight tractor,

pull smaller tools, and travel faster to accomplish the same amount of work." Seventeen years later they decide to build "heavyweight" tractors and convince the farmer to run larger implements.

The new Iron Horses were, in fact, heavier, stronger, and more powerful than the 30 series: All three statements were true. Chronic failures of final drives, transmissions, and some engines had haunted Deere in the 30 series. So the Iron Horse was Deere's classic attempt to market "the same old gal in a new dress," something they are masters of.

IH 86 Series Four-Wheel Drives

With the newly released 86 series out, IH restyled its existing four-wheel drives. The 4366 became the 4386, the 4568 was now the 4586, and a new 350-horsepower model 4786 joined the lineup. As with the previous four-wheel drives, these three models were all made by Steiger, and all three were painted and decaled to be similar in appearance to the 86 series.

The 4386 and 4586 had newly designed wet, multiple disc, externally mounted hydraulic brakes, which were needed to provide more braking power as tractors were increasingly growing in Steiger horsepower. A larger Steiger-designed cab now had the IH data center digital readout monitor, instead of the mechanical drive tachometer. Using this, the operator could push a button to see engine rpm, travel speed, and exhaust gas temperature. A two-stage windshield wiper and optional AM-FM radio were also available.

The 4386 was now equipped with a DTI-466 six-cylinder turbocharged and intercooled diesel engine. This was the first IH farm tractor to use an engine intercooler to cool the intake air entering the engine from the turbocharger.

The 4786 used the DV-800 IH-built eight-cylinder vee-style turbocharged engine. The 4786 could be outfitted with wide single or dual wheels for added traction using row-crop axles with a 4-inch diameter bar. The bar axles permitted wheel tread settings from 68 to 125 inches.

All three 86 series four-wheel drives were restriped in 1979 with the addition of a wing to the front of the decal. This was similar to that of the 88 series 2+2 tractor. The cab roof color was also changed from white to red.

You Get More in a New 84

IH announced a whole new lineup of small row-crop and utility-style tractors in 1978. This new series was called the IH 84 series, and it replaced the older 464-574-674 tractors. The new series was sold under the slogan "You get more in a new 84." The 84 series tractors were assembled at IH's Doncaster, England, assembly plant, using the IH-built and -designed three- and four-cylinder direct-injection diesel engines built at the IH works in Neuss, Germany.

The IH 84 series offered six basic models, with four tractors available in row-crop and six in utility configurations. The 384 Utility (not offered in row-crop configuration), using a four-cylinder BD-154 diesel, delivered 36 PTO horsepower. It was equipped with a 12-gallon fuel tank along with eight forward and two reverse speeds, which made it a tractor for the "smallest farmer." Its bigger brother was Utility model 484, which used a three-cylinder diesel engine that displaced 179 ci and offered 42 PTO horsepower. The 484 came with a three-point hitch, adjustable wide front axle, and a 20-gallon fuel tank.

When "big power" was necessary, the 52 PTO horsepower model 584 and 62 PTO horsepower 684 were the ideal choices. The 584 used a model D-206 engine while the 684 had a D-239 engine, but both offered exceptional power, torque reserve, and fuel economy. A hydrostatic-drive tractor, the Hydro 84, was also part of the series. Because the hydrostatic drive was clutchless and offered infinitely variable speeds and shuttle shifting capability, the Hydro 84 was the ideal tractor-loader model. It was basically identical to the 684 except that an IH-built hydrostatic-drive transmission replaced the eight forward and four reverse speed gear-drive transmission found in the 684. The 584, 684, 784, and Hydro

After purchasing this 1566 tractor, the dealer is spending some time with the customer going over the tractor operator's book. This can be a valuable bible of information and should always be consulted before operating the tractor. A few moments spent going over the manual with a customer can often lead to repeat sales for the dealer and customer. A good operator always consults the operator's manual when a question arises. *Author Collection*

84 were offered in either row-crop or utility versions.

The king of the hill model in the 84 series was the 784. Using an IH D-246 diesel that delivered 65 PTO horsepower, the 784 was ideal for farmers who needed big tractor power in a compact, maneuverable size. A 66-horsepower model 884 was added in 1979. Optional FWA was first offered in 1981, as was an enclosed two-door operator's cab.

The IH 84 series was still similar to the 74 series it replaced, but in a more refined way. The "split deck" control consoles (like the 86 series had) put shifting controls on the left-hand console, with hitch and PTO and hydraulic outlet controls on the right-hand console. This was fine, but just as in the 86 series, IH received a lot of heat about operators running out of arms to con-

trol the tractor. This was especially evident when using the tractor's remote hydraulic valves to operate a front-end loader while also turning and shuttle-shifting one's direction. Seems that sometimes even an octopus operating the tractor would have its tentacles—er, hands—full.

The 84 series offered hydraulic wet disc brakes for easy stopping, hydrostatic power steering for easy turning, and a deluxe cushioned seat that was adjustable for the operator's weight and height for an easy ride. Besides being easy to operate, the 84 series was simple to perform regular maintenance on. A sealed, maintenance-free 12-volt battery powered the electrical system. Dual full-flow throwaway fuel filters and a vertically mounted spin-on–style engine oil filter were standard. The rear-mounted

Parading down this road are the all-new Pro-Ag 86 series IH tractors. Leading the way is the 161-horsepower model 1586, next the 145-horsepower model 1486, 130-horsepower model 1086, 105-horsepower model 986, 104-horsepower model Hydro 186, and the 85-horsepower model 886. The 86 series tractors featured an all-new heavily sound-insulated operator's cab with mid-mount design. The operator was now located 1.5 feet ahead of the rear axle for better visibility and a smoother ride. The 86 series was the first IH tractor to incorporate electronics in it. *Author Collection*

fuel tank put weight were it was needed—on the drive wheels, for extra traction and stability. The tank was easily filled from ground level, without any steps or rails to climb. The front grille lifted out to expose the transmission oil cooler and engine radiator for easy cleaning. The transmission, which doubled as the hydraulic oil reservoir, was easily checked with a handy dipstick located beside the operator's left heel.

The IH-built transmissions featured four speeds in each of two forward ranges (high-low) and four speeds in reverse. The constant mesh gears were fully synchronized for clash-free shifting. Pressure lubrication on all models except the 384 ensured that all gears and bearings stayed oiled and cooled. The inboard planetary final drives put maximum gear reduction close to the load to reduce the driveline's stress and yet still offered maximum crop clearance. The exclusive Dyna Life dry-type clutch was standard on all the 84 series models except the Hydro 84, which had no clutch. A differential lock was also included to keep the operator in control and traction if the tractor encountered muddy or soft areas. The hydraulically engaged PTO was fully independent. The PTO could be "feathered" if needed.

A two-post ROPS was standard equipment on all the 84 series tractors (except the 384), along with a choice of flattop or crown-style rear wheel fenders. Utility tractors used an underslung horizontal muffler and exhaust piping, while the row-crop tractors had a vertically mounted muffler as standard equipment. A category II three-point hitch with torsion bar–sensing draft and position control was standard on all of the 84 series.

Overall, you did get more in an IH 84 series. So much, in fact, that the basic design of the 84 series (minus the hood styling) was still retained in tractor production through the 1990s.

New Engines and New Problems

With Service Bulletin #S-3357, dated October 18, 1976, IH released for service an accessory kit it hoped would

Powered by an IH-built DT-414 turbocharged six-cylinder diesel engine, the 130 PTO horsepower model 1086 was the most popular model of the new Pro Ag series, with nearly 50,000 units made during its 1976 to 1981 production. The 86 series featured a totally new operator's cab that put operator comfort and convenience first. Thousands of 1086s are still being used every day on farms all over the world. *Author Collection*

be installed on all of its 400 series diesel-engine–powered machines. In March 1977, IH added a coolant filter/conditioner to all of the 86 series tractors (except the 886) as standard equipment to combat a problem all wet-sleeved engines have, called cavitation erosion. Throughout the production run of the IH 66 series, IH engineers were finding that the engine sleeves on higher houred machines tended to show signs of severe pitting, sometimes to the point where coolant would enter the engine's crankcase via the eroded hole in the sleeve. The engine development group found that during use, the engine sleeves would develop tiny pits from a process called cavitation erosion, which is another term for the corrosion that occurs on the water side of a cylinder sleeve. It is not limited to any one design or manufacturer.

Cavitation erosion typically occurs like this. During engine operation, as

the piston moves up and down, the sleeve sealed at the bottom by O-rings will vibrate. This vibration causes a tiny vacuum to form on the cylinder sleeve wall as it moves away from the engine coolant surrounding it. The coolant then flows into the void, bringing a pressure difference that creates a tiny bubble. When the pressure in the liquid stabilizes or the bubble moves to an area of higher pressure, it collapses violently. This collapse can induce a stress on the sleeve sidewall which has been measured at more than 60,000 psi. Repeated action by the bubbles will gradually erode the metal sleeve sidewall away, allowing engine coolant to mix with the engine lubricating oil.

To combat cavitation erosion, IH recommended that the engine coolant be serviced on a regular basis as outlined in the owners manual. The owner should also use coolant conditioners and chemical inhibitors to control the

The king of the new 86 series tractors was the 161 horsepower model 1586. Using the same modular transmission as the prior model 1566, the 1586 was still a brute workhorse. By relocating the engine's muffler under the hood, forward visibility was greatly increased. The wide-opening two-door pressurized cab had more than 43.2 square feet of tinted glass for an expansive view in any direction. *Author Collection*

pH factor in the coolant. If the coolant is not serviced, cavitation erosion may occur. To help the farmer get it right, IH engineers developed a pre-charged full-flow coolant conditioner filter, commonly called the water filter. This vertically mounted, spin-on–style filter helped to condition the coolant, and it removed suspended solid particles in the cooling system. It was not, however, a replacement for changing the coolant.

If the coolant is not maintained on a regular basis, rust and scale buildup will occur. While a little scale deposit may look harmless, it is not. Just 1/16 of an inch of scale deposit is equivalent to 4 1/2 inches of cast iron. Nearly all of the engine's heat transfer would be lost if scale and rust were allowed to build up in an engine. Premature engine overheating and/or failure are likely to occur.

The filter was located above the engine oil cooler on most models, and service was recommended every 400 operating hours. Two thumb-turn valves could stop the flow of coolant so the filter element could be changed. If the two valves were not re-

opened again after filter service, the system received zero benefit from the filter.

IH developed a retrofit kit to install the water filter on the older model IH 400 and 300 series wet-sleeved diesel engines. Very few tractors and combines today are not retrofitted with this filter kit. After IH developed its engine water filter kit, nearly every other OEM copied it on its own wet-sleeved diesel engines.

IH gave its famous 400 series engines a tuneup in 1978, and called these "new" engines the B series. Only the DT models (turbocharged versions) were replaced with a new top-mounted breather package. IH changed the crankcase ventilation system from a side-mounted breather (a square box with a tube leading down from it) to a top-mounted breather on the engine's valve cover. This was done to reduce oil carryover through the crankcase breather system. To accomplish this, IH introduced a new Balance Pressure piston design that included a new intermediate piston ring with an increased

ring gap to improve oil consumption. A pressure relief groove between the top and intermediate ring gaps created a larger pressure difference between the areas above and below the top piston ring. This, in turn, created a more positive seal for the top ring against the sleeve wall. Together the new piston and ring design resulted in a significant improvement in engine oil control. IH still used a four-ring piston with three full keystone-style compression rings and a single oil wiper ring.

The wider ring gap allowed more of the combustion gases to enter the crankcase than the older "narrow gap" ring design did. The higher flow of gases required a larger tube to keep internal crankcase pressure at an acceptable level. Whenever a "wide gap" engine is operated, a larger volume of crankcase gases will be seen at the engine breather tube exit. This is normal.

The camshaft and valvetrain were updated in 1981. A larger diameter cam follower tappet was used, along with different push rods and new rocker arm

Preparing a seedbed is fast work with a 1086 IH tractor. The 16 forward and 8 reverse speeds (when equipped with TA) gave you the right speed every time. Quick response hydraulics were always ready for any task. The mid-mount design of the IH control center gave the operator outstanding visibility of the trailing implement. *Author Collection*

Pulling a model 1482 IH Axial Flow combine, this 1086 is harvesting wheat on a bright summer day. The 130 PTO horsepower of the 1086 was ideally matched to the 1482. The operator stayed cool on hot summer days, thanks to the pressurized cab that filtered incoming air twice. The air-conditioning system would even alert the operator if AC coolant levels were low and needed maintenance. *Author Collection*

bridge supports. This was done to improve component part life durability. The easy way to identify if your engine has the wide-lobe camshaft is to look at the crankcase casting number. This is located directly below the engine oil cooler. The part number is 1802340C1 for the wide-lobe models.

2+2 . . . Equals a Whole Lot More

In 1970, IH engineers mated two 1066 final drives together using the transfer case and transmission from a 4166 to form the first prototype of the last totally new tractor design of the twentieth century. This new design combined the ease of handling found in a conventional two-wheel-drive row-crop tractor with an added two more drive wheels: 2+2. This created the first true row-crop four-wheel-drive tractor ever, a 1970s version of the old tandem tractor setups used by many farmers in the late 1950s and 1960s to get a more powerful tractor.

While experiments with prototypes in the early 1970s proved successful, a number of weak points were also exposed in the testing process. IH engineers had to design a totally new articulation joint with a built-in transfer case to power the front axle. They were also unsure as to where to locate the operator's station. Should it be forward of the articulation joint as Steiger and other articulated tractor manufacturers placed it? Or at the rear of the tractor to take advantage of lower tooling costs, as this meant little or no modification had to be done to the drivetrain? Finally the engineers settled on the rearward cab placement, locating the engine ahead of the front drive axle for increased tractor stability, especially with heavy rear-mounted implements.

In January of 1979, IH shocked the ag market by unveiling the all-new IH 2+2 line to its dealers. This was a totally new kind of farm power: It had a new look in tractor design and a whole lot more. A fully enclosed engine compartment with a rollaway front hood, rear-mounted Control Center Cab, and equal-sized drive tires were the characteristic trademarks of the 2+2.

Two models were offered, the 3388 and 3588. The 3388 delivered 130 PTO horsepower from its DT-436B turbocharged diesel engine. The 3588 was the 150 PTO horsepower version with a DT-466B turbocharged diesel engine as its power plant. Both of these 2+2s used a cab and drivetrain based on the 1086 series tractors. In 1980 a 170 PTO horsepower model 3788 was added to the lineup. The 3788 used the cab and drivetrain from a 1586. None of the 2+2s were available without cabs or as open ROPS cabs.

IH Service Bulletin #S-4180, dated February 4, 1981, noted that a revised aspirated muffler was now being used that reduced tractor "whistling." With the old-style muffler, a "whistling" noise was sometimes heard near the high idle speed and throughout the rest of the loaded engine range. The whistling could change with changes in rpms and engine loads. Many owners replaced engine turbochargers only to have the whistle return, but the turbo was not the cause of the noise; the muffler was the culprit. The whistle was merely annoying, and not harmful to the engine or tractor in any way, but the new muffler helped overcome any customer complaints.

The 3588 had such features as 1,000-rpm PTO, 153-gallon fuel tank capacity (with an optional 63-gallon auxiliary tank available), a cab with a heater and air conditioner, a digital readout IH data center, new PPH, hydraulic wet disc brakes, and a rear three-point hitch. The 2+2s also had a choice of 104-inch or 118-inch axles, to get almost any wheel spacing needed along with wedge-lock wheels. The 3388 was essentially equipped the same except for its engine and a dual speed (540–1000) PTO unit. The tractors' engines were fully enclosed, making the tractors look unique and often intimidating to many.

The view from the cab was not any different than that from a conventional IH 86 series row-crop tractor. The hitch and PTO were still directly behind the operator. The view to the front was

The IH model 686 was a popular workhorse for any size farm. Using either a diesel or gasoline engine (shown here), the 686 was well suited for any job. The two-post ROPS and canopy were standard equipment. IH sold over 6,000 of the model 686 during its 1976 to 1980 production. *Author Collection*

With the red-painted cab roof, this IH 4586 still has the old style black hood stripe decal and not the new "Tri Stripe" decal on it yet. The 4586 used a digital data center to keep the operator informed of engine rpms, travel speed, and exhaust gas temperature. *State Historical Society of Wisconsin*

much different, however, because the hood seemed to reach forward forever. Some farmers had a hard time dealing with this. They claimed it would take a 40-acre field to turn the thing around, or you would run into every fenceline with the long nose and clean it out. In reality, the IH 2+2s turned around in a 15.9-foot circle, something a lot of row-crop tractors could not even begin to do. The key to driving the 2+2 was to watch the front wheels. Wherever they went, you went. When approaching a headland and turning, the front nose swung to the side that you would be turning to, while you were still traveling forward. Then the rear half would turn and follow the front. Many operators

could not understand this until they realized they were being pulled, not pushed, through the field. The experience of driving a 2+2 is unique and one that should be experienced.

One problem that IH did have with the long hood on the 2+2 was during shipping. When the 2+2s were loaded onto railcars, the bumping and jostling of the train cars caused the cable-operated hood latch to release, and the hoods would fly off the tractors. After having several missing hood 2+2s arrive at their destination by rail, IH engineers added a simple rubber hold-down latch to each side of the hood. A service bulletin issued to dealers in August 1980 encouraged them to do the same to

2+2s in their area that had experienced hood roll-off during field operation.

All of the new 2+2s were equipped with a closed center hydraulic system. This system operated the hydraulic pump only when there was a demand. The PPH system used a variable displacement piston pump. When the control valves were actuated, the pressure demand of the load was sensed, a signal was sent to the pump, and the pump then delivered the exact amount of oil needed to do the job. If there was no demand, the pump did not run and thus drain horsepower from the tractor. To protect the PPH hydraulic system, a vertically mounted full-flow spin-on oil filter was made standard equipment. This

This 4386 "Tri Stripe" was photographed on the IH dealer lot in Janesville, Wisconsin. Notice the bar-style axles used to mount outer dual wheels and hubs. The 4386 had more than 170 drawbar horsepower. The Tri Stripe 86 series four-wheel drives proved to be IH's last mass-produced four-wheel-drive tractor line. *Author Collection*

filter on the suction side of the hydraulic pump protected it from any harm that could be caused by oil impurities. Another filter on the oil return line offered an added measure of protection.

The PPH system was great in theory, but IH soon was having a rash of 2+2s lose their hydraulics and steering while in the field or, worse yet, on the road. A new, improved piston-style replacement hydraulic pump (valued at over $1,500) solved the problem.

Another problem encountered by IH engineers was the use of dual wheels on the front axle of the tractor. The design of the articulation joint was such that, if dual wheels were used both front and rear, the front outer dual would contact the rear outer dual, causing severe tractor damage. (IH later solved this problem in the Super 70 series tractors by changing the tractor wheelbase and steering cylinder angles.) IH stated in the 2+2 owners manual that if duals were needed they should be used on the rear axle only. The front axle only served to help deliver part of the engine's power to the ground (even though it could not be turned off), and to be able to carry two 300-gallon front-mounted chemical tanks, if needed.

IH was quick to heavily promote the 2+2 to the market. It had no choice, as this was the strangest-looking tractor in a long time. Many people referred to the 2+2s as "anteaters" due to the tractor's long nose. Early advertising by IH was quick to point out that the 2+2 looked different because it was different. Here was the answer for the farmer who needed a two-wheel-drive row-crop tractor with four-wheel-drive traction and flotation. The IH 2+2 had two-wheel performance, plus two more wheels' drive. The unique design of the 2+2 and the superior traction and flotation it offered allowed the farmer to go when others couldn't, due to poor field conditions. You could plant at the optimum time to maximize plant growth potential or pull a spreader in snow that would stop other tractors. The design advantages of the 2+2 provided the operator with top level comfort, even on hills and rough terrain. The forward-mounted engine and the cab located on the rear half provided unequaled balance, stability, and visibility in a row-crop four-wheel drive.

A unique tractor variation of the 2+2 was the Canadian version. This was identical in features to the 2+2s sold in the United States, except that the wheels were painted black, not IH red. How strange.

Many people called the 2+2s funny names when they saw them. They were "funny"-looking tractors. Besides being called "anteaters" in the United States, 2+2s were called "land sharks" or "worms." Down under in Australia they were nicknamed "snoopy." Funny name

or not, the 2+2 left its mark in tractor development unlike any other tractor had.

IH had its first-ever collector edition toy tractor made by the ERTL CO. for the 2+2's introduction. These replicas were sent to every dealer along with the 2+2 promotional kit. The toy tractor articulated just like the real machine and the front axle pivoted too. A molded plastic field mounted on a cardboard display stand allowed the dealer to demonstrate the concept of the 2+2 to the customer in the salesman's office. Today this toy version of the 3588 2+2 is called the First Edition, and is quite valuable to toy collectors, especially if the field and its stand are also with it.

Acceptance of the 2+2 series went over quite well. The 3388 had 2,146

units made, the 3588 had 5,643 units, and the 3788 had 2,496 units from their 1979–1981 production run.

IH Red Power Showdown Days

IH put the 2+2 tractors in the field for side-by-side demonstrations in what would be its last tractor demo programs. IH called these field days the "Red Power Showdown." The purpose of the showdown was not only to sell the 2+2 but the entire IH lineup of tractors. IH even gave away a 2+2 tractor to one lucky farmer whose entry was drawn from all the showdown participants who had registered regionally in 1979. In 1980, IH gave away the free (300-hour) use of an IH 1086 tractor to six lucky winners across the country.

The tractor that had a totally new look (to say the least) was the all new IH 2+2. The 2+2 stood for two-wheel drive handling and turning plus two more wheels' drive. The 2+2 looked different because it was different. Introduced in 1979, the IH 2+2 line included the 130-hosepower model 3588 and 150-horsepower model 3588. It was expanded in 1979 to include the 160-horsepower model 3788. *Author Collection*

The IH 86 series had the side grille panels specially painted red, and they bore a round white circular decal, which read "RED POWER." On the side of the tractor hoods, IH placed a Branding Iron decal. This was a decal of a cattle-branding iron from the old West with a freshly "burned" IH mark next to the red-hot iron. The marketing department at IH had a field day with this theme, telling people to go to the showdown days and "make IH your brand!" IH had planned to build 2,500 of the 86 series as RED POWER Demo tractors.

In the first year of the RED POWER Showdown program (1978), IH gave away eight tractors to the lucky winners in a national drawing. Grand prize was a 1586; there were two second prizes of 484 tractors, and third prizes of five Cadet 81 lawn tractors. In 1979, IH again offered a Red Power Showdown program with even better prizes. The Grand prize was an IH 2+2, second prize was an 886, and there were four third prizes of 484 Utility tractors. The 2+2 made the ideal grand prize, as it was the showcased tractor of the showdown. These were some really nice prizes to win just for attending a tractor demo show.

Using side-by-side comparisons of the IH 2+2 to Deere or other makes during the Showdown Days quickly showed the superior traction and flotation of the 2+2. Even competitive FWA tractors still showed their weaknesses when run beside the 2+2. Sometimes the 2+2 even outperformed the IH 86 series in the field.

New Hydraulics in an Old Chassis

In 1980, IH engineers added a new variable displacement piston-type hydraulic pump to the IH 86 series. The use of this new piston pump now allowed the operator to have variable oil flow at the rear outlets. These new 86 series tractors with the PPH system were easily identified by their red-painted side panels next to the grille and the small red pinstripe above the black stripe on the side of the hood and cab

This photo of a 3588 2+2 pulling an IH offset disk harrow shows something that IH did not recommend: using dual wheels on the front axle of the tractor. The reasoning behind this was twofold: the outer wheels could contact the cab when turning, and the front axle was not rated for the use of dual wheels. *Author Collection*

Red Power Buyer's Choice

Model	Red Edge Rebate	Free Cub Cadet	Red Power Dollars
4386, 4586, 4786 4WD Tractors	$3,500	19 hp Cub Cadet 982 $4,885 value	$4,500
All 2+2s	$3,000	17 hp Cub Cadet 782 $4,225 value	$3,900
1586	$2,500	16 hp Cub Cadet 682 $3,295	$3,200
1086, 186 Hydro, 1486	$2,000	16 hp Cub Cadet 582 $2,880 value	$2,600
786, 886, 986	$1,500	482 $2,465	$2,000

doors. They are commonly referred to as the "Tri Stripe" 86s.

While the variable displacement system of hydraulic power was new to the 86 series, it had been previously used in the 30 series 2+2s, with mixed success.

Another feature of the PPH 86 series was the multicolored hydraulic flow control levers on the lower right-hand console of the cab, and the use of newly shaped shifting lever grips called "pistol grip knobs." All true PPH IH 86 series have an extra spin-on–type hydraulic oil filter mounted under the left-hand frame rail to filter the hydraulic oil from the tractor's oil cooler.

The engine received a slight "tuneup" too. An optional aspirated air cleaner was now available on all the 86 series models except the 786 and 886. An aspirated air cleaner uses suction power from the engine's exhaust to remove dirt and dust from the air cleaner before it can plug the filter. This pre-cleaning extended the life of the engine's air cleaner. To make the aspirated air cleaner work properly, the exhaust pipe size was increased from 3 inches to 3.5 inches in diameter. A pipe with a curved tip replaced the straight pipe with weather cap.

The drivetrain also received a "tuneup." After many complaints from customers about the shifting levers binding and galling (and sometimes even cutting themselves in half due to severe use), the levers were redesigned. By angling the levers more rearward, the operator could now enter and exit the left-hand door without getting caught on the levers. Engineers increased the cab's opening side windows in height, which offered even more side visibility.

The tractor's air-conditioning system received an overhaul, too. IH switched from the conventional "flare"-style A-C lines and compressor fittings to a new O-ring–style fitting system designed to give better leak protection.

The operator's environment was also enhanced with the 1981 models. Inside the cab, a new hydraulically cushioned, high-back operator's seat made driving the 86 series even more comfortable. Now the 86 series had the same high level of interior comfort as the 2+2 did. A new optional Western interior trim dressed up the interior in buckskin tan, and it included LED readout AM-FM multiplex radio with cassette tape player. This new Western interior now gave the farmer three interior choices: standard, burgundy, and western trim levels.

To help sell iron in 1981, IH offered farmers its "Red Power Buyers Choice." This gave the customer three choices when purchasing a new IH tractor. A buyer could choose from a new Cub Cadet garden tractor, Red Edge instant

How do you build a 2+2? Put two tractors together, that's how. By using a modified rear half of an IH 86 series, and a new front frame assembly that put the engine ahead of the front axle (for balance), the 2+2 was born. Here a skilled crane operator at Farmall Works joins the two halves of a 2+2 together. *Author Collection*

IH exported many tractors to other countries including Australia, Germany, and the United Kingdom. To ship these machines, IH had the tractors mounted on large skids. Here a pair of 3588s is being loaded for export onto a waiting ship. The cab windows were covered with protective wraps to guard against damage. *State Historical Society of Wisconsin*

cash rebate, or Red Power savings dollars (good toward the purchase of any new IH equipment or parts).

Even after all of the hype about having a "power saving" hydraulic system on its machines, IH still went back to the old school and built a production run of the "open center" hydraulic tractors after the PPH tractors were built. It turned out that the PPH hydraulic system was not anywhere near as advantageous as

IH had expected. In some cases an old open center 86 series would outperform a PPH tractor.

Once again IH was playing catch-up with the competition. It had an answer to the problem, but it seemed IH never spent enough time on testing the solution. A few of the aftermarket "will fitter" parts suppliers even went as far as to offer kits to convert your PPH tractor back to the old open center system. A

number of the 86s had this done to them in the field as an alternative to the PPH's constant pump troubles. Converting back to the open center system was fine to get you going, but now the use of the flow control that PPH offered was locked out.

At the same time IH introduced the "Tri Stripe" 86 series in 1980, it also shuffled a couple of tractor models around. The 886, which had had a

Whether it be primary, secondary, or final tillage, the 2+2 let you farm when other tractors would not. The superior balance and traction of the 2+2 design allowed the tractor to "float" over soft spots. And because the 2+2 had equal-sized drive tires, the tractor had a larger footprint than a conventional row-crop tractor. *Author Collection*

Previous pages
Plowing or planting, haying or harvesting, the 2+2 was truly a tractor for all seasons. The unique design of a row-crop tractor combined with an articulated four-wheel drive was, ironically, never copied by IH's competitors. *Author Collection*

D-360 American diesel engine as its power plant, was switched to the German-built D-358 diesel. The 886 was now a 90-horsepower rated tractor.

IH introduced a new economy model tractor called the 786, which used the D-358 German-built six-diesel engine. This engine was a six-cylinder, naturally aspirated, direct injection engine, which turned out 80 PTO horsepower in Nebraska Tractor Test #1388. The 786 was available as either an open platform or four-post ROPS only, but did not have an enclosed operator's cab.

The main reason IH came out with the 786 was to replace the 686 and Hydro 86 models, which had just been dropped from the lineup, and to combat the sale of the John Deere 2840 and 2940 and the Ford 7700 in the South. The 786, along with the competitor models, was a low-priced budget tractor that had few options and sold at an economical price. Ironically, it became quite popular in the dairy farm industry too. IH built only 1,844 786s in its one-year production run. Neither the 886 nor 786 was offered with the PPH hydraulic system.

IH even built some "Special Order" 86 series tractors. One of these special edition tractors was called the Taco Special. The Taco Special was an IH 86 series tractor that had special tires, no TA, no ROPS, or other equipment. It was intended to be delivered to the Republic of Mexico but none were never shipped. This series was made up of 886, 986, 1086, and 1486 IH tractor models. A total of 2,815 Taco Specials were built by IH.

The regular IH 86 series tractors were strong sellers. Here are the total numbers of each model made:

- 786: 1,844
- 886: 9,578
- 986: 20,554
- 1086: 47,420
- 1486: 21,117
- 1586: 13,636

These numbers clearly show that 100- to 150-horsepower tractors were the size to be buying in the later 1970s.

While IH offered a warmed-over version of the 86 series (in its PPH models) as "new" tractors in 1980, John Deere was still selling its tired, warmed-over "Generation II" (Iron Horse) tractors. IH was not about to lie down and get run over by a herd of horses, however. It had long ago set its sights on overtaking Deere in the tractor market. Judgment day was here, and IH had its deck stacked. There was a new number one in town.

Chapter 4
The 1980s
END OF AN ERA

*T*he farm economy of the 1970s was about to change drastically in the 1980s. IH (which had just survived a major strike in 1979) was ready to ramp up production to pre-strike levels. The dealer network was in need of some machinery inventory to replace the items it had sold during the strike, but IH was planning on increasing production over the pre-strike levels. Interest rates were on the rise, and the United States had imposed a grain embargo against the USSR. The farm economy was still stable, but a major change unlike that ever seen before was about to take place. Many factors coming to a head would finally cause IH to self-destruct in the 1980s, taking many dealers down with it.

"The New Number One": The IH 50 Series

In September of 1981, IH called its ag dealer network to a meeting in Kansas City, Missouri, for a major announcement. At the dealer meeting themed "New Leadership Meeting" IH was ready to unveil a bold new design. Jim Bostic, vice president of IH agricultural equipment marketing, stated, "We must work together to achieve a competitive edge in the marketplace, never losing sight of our primary mission: to create a higher level of customer satisfaction than our competition." A totally new tractor (code named the TR4 by IH engineering at Hinsdale) was unveiled at that dealer meeting that would forever change IH's (and many other brands') tractor designs. IH announced the 50 series row-crop tractors. Three totally new tractors that would meet the needs of the farmer for today and tomorrow.

At this dealer meeting held in Kansas City, IH spent over $1.2 million to introduce the "New Number One." It allotted another $325,000 for advertising, along with $365,000 for parts and service training. Officials estimated that testing the tractors at Nebraska would run $50,000 per tractor. This was not a cheap undertaking by IH.

Several other new IH tractors were introduced at the Kansas City New Leadership dealer meeting. These tractors included the 3288 and 3688 row-crop tractors, the 6388, 6588, and 6788 improved 2+2 series, and the 7388, 7588, and 7788 articulating four-wheel drives. Also new were the 234, 244, and 254 low horsepower compact diesel tractors. Newly styled and improved were the 84 series utility and row-crop tractors, including the 274 offset (which replaced the retired 140 model) and the economy class 383 and 483 tractors.

The all-new IH tractor lineup for 1981 included (clockwise from top) 3088 (81 horsepower), 3688 (112 horsepower), 5288 (162 horsepower), 5088 (136 horsepower), and 5488 (185 horsepower). All five models featured new right-hand control consoles and were the first U.S.-built IH tractors to use mainly metric fasteners in them. *Author Collection*

View of the right-hand control console of the 50 series. Notice the two shifting levers (speed lever has "Z" shift pattern, while range lever has an "H" pattern) that are easy for the operator to reach. The color-coded remote hydraulic valve control levers was later updated for better operator ergonomics. *Author Collection*

After a major overhaul of the IH tractor lineup was presented to the dealers, the closing session of the meeting ended on this note: "Let's make this partnership work to gain the competitive edge. It's our turn to be number one again." This is exactly why IH had spent millions of dollars and tens of thousands of man-hours developing the new IH 50 series tractors—The "New Number One."

The IH 50 series was IH's last (and sometimes called best) new row-crop tractor series made. The familiar numbering system of prefix numbers 1 through 15 was abandoned. There were three new models of the "New Number One" 50 series. The TX-201, more commonly known as the 5088, rated at 135 PTO horsepower; the TX-200-1 known as the 5288, and rated at

160 PTO horsepower; and the largest IH row-crop tractor ever made, the TX-200-2, referred to as the 5488, and rated at 185 PTO horsepower. IH started the initial designing process in 1976 by asking customers what they wanted in a tractor. After spending over $29.7 million to complete this series' engineering and development, it turned out IH had listened to the customer and responded.

A totally new synchronized 18-speed transmission was IH's answer to the customers who wanted an easy-to-shift transmission. A fully synchronized constant-mesh helical-cut gear transmission could be shifted into any of 18 uniformly spaced forward gears without grinding or gear clash. There were even six reverse speeds. Three ranges (with six gears in each range) were ide-

ally matched to every job. Typically, the low range would be used for PTO work, medium for most field tasks, and high for transport. Each of the six speed gears was uniformly spaced about 17 percent apart with no overlap, so the operator always had the right gear—not too slow or too fast.

The new transmission was equipped with a mid-mounted wet master clutch. This was tested over 10,000 full load cycles with no signs of wear. Tests indicated this would provide more than twice the life of a dry-type clutch. This new wet-type multiple disc clutch was engaged by a hydraulic assistance cylinder attached to the clutch pedal, and it needed only 15 pounds of pressure to engage or disengage. The master clutch was located between the speed and range transmissions. No other competitor offered a mid-mount design, which was easy to service and made maximum use of engine input torque. The clutch was constantly bathed in cool, filtered hydraulic oil and automatically feathered and cushioned for easy, smooth starts. IH also designed the growing option of FWA into the 50 series. The front-axle driveshaft exited the transmission in the lower center of the speed transmission housing, which allowed the driveshaft to go directly to the front axle without the need for expensive transfer cases and multiple U-joint driveshafts.

Surrounding this new clutch was a totally new 18-speed synchronized transmission called the Synchro Tri-Six, or STS. Six gears, along with three new working ranges (low, medium, and high), provided a new level of operation. A new computer monitoring system called a Sentry was used to monitor several transmission functions. If for any reason the hydraulic oil pressure dropped in the transmission, the Sentry would automatically shut down the oil-cooled clutches to avoid any heat or friction damage. By simply shifting down one gear, or to another range or reverse, the operator could reset the Sentry. An indicator light on the dash warned the operator when the Sentry system was being activated. This was

With an IH-built model DTI-466 C engine cranking out 185 PTO horsepower, this 5488 easily handles its fully mounted two-way plow in sod. Dual rear wheels provide better traction and flotation. *Author Collection*

the first computer intelligence added to a farm tractor.

Shifting on the 50 series was partly controlled through the use of electric switches and solenoids that operated multidisc wet-type clutches in the speed transmission. Two clutches were used alternately to provide clash-free shifting: A simple "Z" shifting pattern allowed for power shifting between one and two, three and four, and five and six gears. When shifting to any other gears, the clutch pedal had to be depressed. Full load power-shifts, either up or down, could be easily accomplished by moving the speed selection lever sideways. The three-range transmission was controlled by a range shift lever with a simple "H"

pattern. Low range and reverse were located directly across from each other for easy shuttle shifting when used for loader work, and all of the STS transmission controls were located on the right-hand side in a console. The continued use of pistol grip-styled shifting grips (from the late 86 series) shaped to fit the operator's hand, combined with a simple shift pattern, were easy to master. IH used helical-cut CNC precision-machined gears throughout the STS transmission for quieter operation and clash-free shifting.

The use of massive cast-iron transmission and rear-end housings along with inboard planetary gear final reduction drives helped deliver the power

and unmatched torque from the famous IH 400 series six-cylinder engines to the ground. Modular component design of the speed, range, and final drive housings made for easy service and transmitted power more efficiently. Maintenance costs are also greatly reduced, as the entire transmission need not be disassembled, just the component needing repair could be removed. Wet multidisc brakes and an electrically operated differential lock were standard equipment. A dual shaft independent PTO unit equipped with two speeds (540 and 1,000 rpm) was standard on the 5088, while a single-shaft (1,000 rpm only) was offered on the 5288 and 5488. The PTO was now hydraulically

Maintenance is a snap on the IH 50 series, thanks to wide, easy-opening service doors. The top air screen opens for access to the radiator and transmission oil cooler. Two wide-opening doors on the engine compartment make engine oil-level checks and filter changes easy. *Author Collection*

controlled, unlike previous series, which had used a mechanical linkage.

A look at the front end of the IH 50 series showed a very radical departure from the traditionally styled IH tractors of previous series. Gone were the silver bar grille, twin headlights, and familiar white side panels. Now a new red boxy metal hood and totally enclosed engine were prominent features. Two swing-out side doors (one on each side) allowed the operator to perform daily service tasks with ease, and enclosing the engine

helped keep its heat and noise away from the operator and complemented the new smooth, stylish hood lines.

Cooling air for the engine's radiator was drawn through the top of the hood and expelled out the front grille, away from the tractor. This was called Forward Air Flow, and was a new solution to an old problem, creating lower cab and engine compartment temperatures through engine-cooling airflow. The problem of the radiator grille screen getting plugged was also eliminated, as was

that of the dust blow-back commonly associated with conventional cooling fans that blew hot air over the engine and toward the operator. In the new system, a six-bladed fan located ahead of the radiator drew hot engine-compartment air and dust around the radiator and blew it out the front of the tractor. After the tractor was shut off, any chaff or debris on the top-mounted air-intake screens simply blew off.

IH actually field-tested two versions of a cooling system in the 50 series. The first version used a conventional engine-mounted fan that sucked cooling air in through the front grille and blew it over the engine (just as the previous 86 series and all other IH tractors had). The enclosed hood that IH had designed caused severe engine overheating because the hot engine air was trapped in a "tin box" and had no route for escape. This also made operator cab temperatures rise, and severely affected the tractor cab's air-conditioning performance.

The second version called an R-A-F (reverse airflow) was the type that pulled cool air in from the top of the hood and "pushed" it out the front of the tractor. The engine's cooling fan was mounted ahead of the radiator oil cooler and A-C condenser unit. This virtually eliminated radiator plugging. If any debris or field chaff would plug the air intake screens, the operator would quickly see, as they were located on the top of the tractor's hood in plain sight. IH had developed the Forward Air Flow that would become a trademark on the other IH tractors introduced in the 1980s.

IH still used the reliable 400 series six-cylinder inline diesel engines as the tractor's power source. These engines, made in IH's Melrose Park assembly plant, were field proven and well known for their durability and unmatched torque rise. The 5088 used a model DT436B engine, while the 5288 had a DT466B, and the 5488 featured a DTI466B. All three engines were six-cylinder turbocharged diesels, with the DTI466B having an engine intercooler added, thus bringing the letter I into the engine model designation. Later in the 50 series production run, the 5488's DTI466B would be upgraded to the "C" series engine. The "C" series had an increased capacity engine oil pump, wider engine bearings, and an inline Bosch fuel-injection pump for better power response.

The Power Priority hydraulic system used three pumps to produce a total flow of 67 gallons per minute. This closed-center style of hydraulic system had been used successfully earlier on the 2+2 series and the late 86 series. The heart of the Power Priority system was a variable-displacement hydraulic pump, which only operated when needed, and supplied the exact flow required to do the job. The three hydraulic pumps were all mounted externally on the tractor's right side for easy service (if needed). Multiple full-flow hydraulic filters on the pumps' suction side stopped harmful contaminants before damage could occur. Cab flow controls to the remote hydraulic valve outlets offered a new level of operator control. Up to four remote outlets with breakaway couplers could be ordered, and the matching, color-coded controls in the cab and at the outlets made hookups easy and right the first time. They could be coupled or uncoupled under pressure.

Matching the performance of the new hydraulic system was the three-point hitch, which offered 7,000 pounds lift on the 5088 and over 8,000 pounds lift on the 5288 and 5488. This could easily handle the toughest implements. IH offered a new claw-style hitch for the 50 series: Instead of using an arm assembly with a ball in the arm, it has the ball mounted to the implement. The claw hooks are placed under them, and as the hitch is raised, the balls slide into place. This was ideal for one-person hitching jobs. It sounded like a modern-day IH "Fast Hitch."

The two-door IH-built Control Center Cab was still rubber ISO-mounted and basically unchanged from the 86 series. The exception was that all of the hydraulic and transmission controls were now on the right-hand console, not split like the 86 series controls were.

IH tractors used in planting operations are sometimes outfitted with large liquid chemical tanks, such as these shown here on this 5288. When designing, IH engineers needed to consider the load their tractors carried, such as the one here. *Author Collection*

IH 7388 four-wheel-drive tractor SN#502 owned by Stuart and Shirley Johnson of Rushville, Nebraska. This is one of two such units known to exist, and it has many features that were introduced on the Steiger Series IV tractors a few years later. The side engine covers tip up to reveal a turbocharged and intercooled IH 466-ci six-cylinder diesel engine that produces over 230 horsepower. *Author Collection*

IH even offered three interior choices: The standard black interior could be replaced by the optional burgundy (red) interior or Western (buckskin tan) interior. All three interiors offered a hydraulic-suspension cloth seat, a heater, an air conditioner, and AM-FM radio.

IH was so confident in the quality and performance of the new 50 series tractors that all of them came with industrywide, unprecedented three-year or 2,500-hour extended warranties of the engine and tractor drivetrain. This long-term warranty could be accomplished by using more than 1,000 checks of factory quality-control measures and inspections. These measures and checks were performed at all steps of the manufacturing processes. Other competitors would later offer multiyear warranties on their tractors, but IH had once again set the industry benchmark.

Even after IH put all these great new features into their tractor, it still needed to sell it. To do this, it hired Doerfer Division of CCA (an independent testing firm) to run side-by-side tests using the IH 5288 and a John Deere 4640 quad range. The tests were conducted in the same field, using identical implements. The IH 50 series beat the Deere in both acres-per-gallon-of-fuel used and acres-per-hour worked. The IH 50 series worked over 5.6 percent more acres-per-gallon in both disking and chisel plowing. While disking, the IH 50 series also worked an average of 10.5 percent more acres-per-hour. With more acres worked and less fuel used, IH had field proved that it had the "New Number One."

IH invited 57 owners of John Deere 4640 and 4440 tractors to evaluate the new 50 series at the IH Engineering Center in Hinsdale, Illinois, during June of 1981. In the majority of 27 key areas, they rated the IH 50 series better than their own Deere. A full 74 percent of Deere owners preferred the all-new IH Synchro Tri-Six transmission shifting to their Deere. The new IH mid-mounted master clutch was rated easier to use by 60 percent of the test participants. In the cab area, 84 percent of test participants found IH's digital readouts superior to Deere gauges. Overall, 50 of 57 John Deere owners rated the IH 50 series over their own. IH had built a "New Number One!"

Proving the 50 series through independent field tests was fine for some, but the real test of a tractor took place at the Nebraska Tractor Test in Lincoln. These unbiased tests were all run under similar conditions, testing the same features. They measured fuel economy (measured in horsepower hours per gallon of fuel), drawbar pull, and PTO performance. IH sent each model of the new 50 series to Nebraska for testing. The 5488 (tested from May 26 to June 8, 1982) set new records, not only for IH tractors, but also for the entire industry to meet!

The 5488 used fewer pounds of fuel per horsepower hour than any other two-wheel-drive tractor over 165 PTO horsepower ever tested at Nebraska. It also recorded 18,646 pounds of drawbar pull, another record, and developed 164.82

Nebraska Tractor Tests: 1981-1982

Model	Engine	Test No.	PTO Power
5088	DT-436B Diesel	1419	136
5288	DT-466B Diesel	1420	163
5488	DTI-466C Diesel	1441	187
5000	DT-466C Diesel	Experimental	200+
5188	DT-436B Diesel	Experimental	125

drawbar horsepower. This was more than any other two-wheel drive tractor tested had ever developed. Of course, IH marketing was quick to capitalize on these findings. It published a special brochure of these findings to help sell the "New Number One."

Some of the improvements IH made to the 50 series over its relatively short production life included an improved Sentry monitoring system, larger bearings on the engine cooling fan shaft, replacement of the park lock cable with a solid rod, and a major speed transmission update. The speed transmission update was done to counter problems incurred during high cycles of maximum loading on the shifting clutches. IH engineers found that the fine splines on the transmissions shafts and gears could "round over" during heavy use, causing the tractor to be immovable. The solution was to use coarse-splined shafts and gears that would not round over. An update package was developed for retail units that had experienced this failure. All of the 50 series made after 1983 had the new updated transmission in them.

Many dealers found unique ways to sell the 50 series. One IH dealer (the former Martinson Implement of Brooklyn, Wisconsin) held an IH Red Power Showdown Tractor Demonstration Day to show the new IH 50 series to its customers. One of the tests that the dealership set up for participants was the "stump test." The sales staff set a glass of water on a tree stump. The tractor operator was to back up to the stump and tip the glass of water (using the tractor's drawbar) so that only part of it would spill into an adjacent empty pail. The purpose of this test was to show how smooth the new IH 50 series clutch was compared to anything else on the market. Those who took the stump test achieved nearly a 95 percent success rate by not spilling a drop more than was required.

While IH did not set any sales records with the 50 series, it did produce 8,176 units of the 5088, 5,905 units of the 5288, and 3,951 units of the big 5488 tractor. Not too bad, considering the

plummet in farm equipment sales due to the economy.

The next generations of the IH 50 series never made it the dealer's showroom. The first variation used the newly developed IH Vari-Torque transmission, which replaced the six-speed gearbox used in the 50 series with a variable speed, hydro-mechanical unit. This was the product of combining a hydrostatic-drive transmission with a gear-drive unit. The engine's power was split upon entering the speed transmission. Part of the power load was transmitted through a gear-drive pack, and part was put through a hydrostatic-drive unit. The power was joined together again before exiting this housing and continuing on to the three-speed range transmission. The unique feature of the Vari-Torque was that it offered the efficiency of a gear

drive with the variable speed features of a hydro. The operator could choose any one of three ranges (high-medium-low) and have infinitely variable speeds in each range. Ironically, this type of transmission was tested by IH in the 1950s both in Europe and the United States. The Vari-Torque tractor still used the 50 series Control Center and front styling. At least one new tractor model was to be introduced in 1985 with Vari-Torque. This is believed to be the model 5188.

The other new tractor (code named TX189) was also to still retain the Forward Air Flow cooling the 50 series had had, along with its sheet-metal styling. The major change here was to the cab and the transmission: The right-hand door cab on the 50 series was eliminated, and a new flat control console was installed on the right-hand side of

The 113 PTO horsepower model 3688 shown here is equipped with the optional FWA drive axle made by Elwood Mfg. The FWA option gave greater traction in soft or muddy field conditions. *Author Collection*

Studio shot of the 112 PTO horsepower model 3488 Hydro. IH built just over 400 of these tractors during its 1981 to 1985 production run. This would be IH's last hydrostatic-drive tractor. Finding a 3488 tractor today is a rare occurrence. *Author Collection*

Three years later, in 1987, the TX189 tractor (which IH was ironically going to call the "New Farmall") was announced to the public in a slightly modified form called the Magnum 7100 series tractor.

The "Never Made" IH 7388, 7588, and 7788 Four-Wheel Drives

At the dealer meeting in Kansas City when the 50 series tractors were introduced, IH also unveiled its new four-wheel-drive tractors. These were to be built by the Steiger Tractor Co. of Fargo, North Dakota, using IH-built engines and drive axles, with Steiger-supplied frames and cabs, as was the case in the previous model 86 series four-wheel drives. These three new models in the 70 series four-wheel drives directly replaced the previous 86 series four-wheel drives. The smallest tractor (7388) was powered by a DTI466B engine rated at 230 horsepower—an IH-built, six-cylinder 466-ci turbocharged and intercooled engine. The two bigger models, the 280-horsepower 7588 and 330-horsepower 7788, each used the IH-built V-800 turbocharged V-8 diesel engine. The 7588 and 7788 shared common driveline components with each other, while the smaller 7388 was unique onto itself.

All three models used sheet-metal styling designed to copy the 50 series look with similar decal striping. The cabs were changed from the previous 86 series four-wheel-drive models in that the interior layout design and control locations were similar to the new Steiger Series IV tractors that would be introduced in 1982. A few of the new features were tilt/telescoping steering, new right-hand-console-located controls, newly designed cab heating and air-conditioning systems, and a new cab fresh-air intake system that was copied from Steiger.

One unique feature was the side engine-access panels. Instead of opening to the rear as the 50 series did, these panels lifted at the bottom edge and were pushed up and out, over the operator's head—somewhat like a garage door in reverse. Stuart Johnson of Rushville, Nebraska, who owns two

the operator's seat. The left-hand door was relocated from the "A" post to the "B" post. This made the doors hinge open from the rear B cab post, instead of the front A post as they had in the 86 and 88 series. With the door opening being reversed, the operator did not need to "climb" the rear tires when entering. This new cab design was code-named the C-88.

The engine throttle control was relocated to the right-hand console for easier operation, and the single shifting lever was also reconfigured for the shorter throw pattern. This new console was needed to "clean up" the interior of the cab. New electronic controls and monitoring systems were to be used in place of analog gauges.

Newly revised hydraulic control levers were easier to reach, due to their angled alignment to the operator, rather

than being perpendicular, as they were in the 50 series. The PTO control lever and rear hitch position levers were also to be relocated for easier operation. Another item that was to be changed was the diesel fuel tank fill location. The choice of interior trim levels and colors was to be changed, too. And finally, the differential lock control was to be upgraded to a style similar to that found on the Deere product. Directly below the revised cab was the new 18-speed Full Powershift transmission.

Both of these tractors were caught in a "Bermuda Triangle," however, when IH's sale of its Ag division was announced. On that day the employees at the Hinsdale, Illinois, Engineering Center loaded the TX189, covered with a tarp, and hauled it to Racine, Wisconsin. The fate of the Vari-Torque 5188 is still unknown to this author today.

The 150 PTO horsepower model 6588 2+2 is the ideal match to an IH 4800 field cultivator. The powerful IH-built six-cylinder turbocharged diesel engine has a high torque reserve to pull through the toughest area in a field without shifting gears. *Author Collection*

7388s (SN#501 and #502), leaves his engine panels off for two reasons. First, he doesn't want them to fall off and be run over by the machine, and second, it lowers the engine compartment temperature. The engine cooling air is still pulled in from the front, but with the side panels on it can only escape under the cab or below the engine. One can only wonder that if IH had built the 88 series four-wheel drives, would they have experienced higher than normal engine temperatures because of the stylish panels?

The totally new hydraulic pump (manufactured by the Commercial Shearing Pump Co.) was mounted directly in front of the engine to the crankshaft. The pump had dual pumping chambers to supply more hydraulic oil to the tractor. One chamber was able to meet the needs of the remote circuits exclusively, while the other supplied the lube oil, steering, and other hydraulic functions.

IH printed a single sheet of literature on the 70 series four-wheel drives. Upon examination of the sheet, it appeared to many that the tractor in the black-and-white photo had been retouched or faked. Conversely, it was held to be true by many others that the tractor in the spec sheet was real and untouched. The only other time the 70 series four-wheel drives were illustrated on an IH advertisement was when the entire 1982 IH tractor lineup was depicted in an artist's drawing on (ironically) the last full line tractor poster IH would issue to its dealers. This poster is quite rare today, and can be very valuable to collectors.

If the literature picture looks "faked" and no one has seen these four-wheel drives at dealer lots, it would be safe to assume that IH just never made these tractors even though they intended to do so. Were they secret tractor testing

Transporting the IH 1482 pull-type Axial Flow combine is fast when the 6588 2+2 is involved. The 6588's four-wheel braking system allows for quick, sure stops if you need them. The tight turning of the 2+2 allows easy access to narrow field roads. *Author Collection*

models? The public knew them by their model number designation, but to IH they also had a Tractor eXperimental (TX) number, just as all IH tractor prototypes do. The 7388 was known as TX 202, the 7588 was called TX 203, and the 7788 was known as TX 204.

IH engineers designated a particular unit using these TX codes. This was their code for identifying the various versions of a tractor they were testing. The corporate naming committee and product identification committee decided the final model numbers/names that would be used for sales and marketing of the tractors.

IH never had the 70 series tested at Nebraska, thus it may be easy to think the tractors were never made. Many people believed this to be true until recently, when a number of these tractors were discovered. In reality, it turned out that IH had built at least two of each model offered, the difference being in that one tractor was equipped with a three-point hitch and the other had only a drawbar, often called a "bareback" tractor. None of the IH 70 series were ever tested at Nebraska.

IH decided to sell its stock interest in the Steiger Tractor Co. in 1982 to generate some badly needed cash. The company's interest in Steiger was sold to the German tractor company called Deutz. Another factor behind the sale was IH's inability to add a rear PTO and some kind of a power-shift transmission. IH's 4WD-market share had been slowly eroding away. It was now at about 12 percent (less than half) of what it had been in 1976. After this sale took place, and because the market for four-wheel-drive tractors had come nearly to a complete stop, IH decided to liquidate the 70 series four-wheel drives before production even started. All three model sizes were sold "as is" to the highest IH dealer bidder at the Hinsdale Engineering Center auction. This ended IH's lineup of large articulating four-wheel drives, just over 20 years since the first 4300 four-wheel drive was built.

The IH 30 Series Row-crop Tractors

While the IH 50 series replaced the higher horsepower row-crop tractors, IH still needed to satisfy the needs of the

The IH 274 offset tractor is shown here cultivating. Because the operator has a clear view of the row-crop in front of him, high value crops are not easily damaged by the "cultivator blight" that may be caused by blind spots with other tractors. *Author Collection*

controls were now located on the right-hand cab console. An electric solenoid (actuated by the operator moving the speed gearshift lever) controlled the transmission's TA on the 3088, 3288, and 3688. This still offered the operator 16 forward and 8 reverse speeds, ideally spaced for top production in the feedlot or field. The range lever used an H pattern like the 86 series had; however the speed lever had a Z shift pattern similar to that of the 50 series. The electric-controlled TA eliminated the cable and mechanical linkages used on prior model tractors to control the TA. Longer TA life could be expected as the linkage could not "come out of adjustment." A hydraulic-powered transmission brake delivered super smooth shifting between ranges. An all-wheel-drive attachment manufactured by Elwood Co. was used for improved traction and was available as optional equipment for all 30 series tractors.

A Hi-Clearance model of the 3688 was also built by IH in very limited numbers. This allowed growers of bedded and specialty crops an additional 18 inches of ground clearance. The poor farm economy, coupled with a $51,000+ price tag for a 3688 Hi-Clearance, surely hindered sales. 3688 Hi-Clearance tractors today are quite rare, as only a few hundred must have been made.

The very, very low production of the model 3488 hydrostatic-drive tractor was primarily due to the stagnant U.S. farm economy. IH built 213 units in 1981. Only one 3488 Hydro tractor was built in 1982. Production rebounded in 1983 to 105 units and 146 tractors were built in 1984–85. The 3488 Hydro had a list price of over $49,000, while the previous model 186 Hydro had a list price of $33,000. No wonder the 3488 did not sell well. Today the 3488 Hydro tractor, of which only 465 units altogether were built, is a rarity.

The Power Priority hydraulic system used on the 50 series was also offered as standard equipment on the 3688 and 3488 Hydro. The digital data center gave the operator instant digital readout of engine rpm, travel speed, exhaust gas temperature, and PTO speed. This was offered

lower horsepower tractor market. The answer was the IH 30 series (code-named TR3A). The 80-horsepower model 3088, the 90-horsepower model 3288, the 112-horsepower hydrostatic-drive model 3488, and the 113-horsepower 3688 constituted the 30 series lineup. These "small brothers" to the 50 series shared the same exterior styling and forward engine-cooling airflow as

the 50 series. But underneath the cosmetic sheet-metal work was the same basic drivetrain that had been used on the prior models 786, 886, and Hydro 186 and 986, which they replaced. IH estimated the total engineering expense of the TR3A to be $3.3 million.

The major difference in the new 30 series tractors was that all of the transmission, PTO, hitch, and hydraulic

Nebraska Tractor Tests: 1980-1984

Model	Engine	Test No.	PTO Power
3088	D-358 Diesel	1551	81
3288	D-360 Diesel	1438	90
3488 Hydro	D-466 Diesel	1439	112
3988	D-436 Diesel	Never built	???
3688	D-436 Diesel	1440	113

as standard on the 3488 Hydro, and optional on the 3288 and 3688. A dual shaft PTO (540–1,000 rpm) that was hydraulically actuated for smooth engagement and disengagement was standard on all 30 series tractors.

It is somewhat confusing that IH did not introduce all of the 30 series models at one time. At the dealer meeting in Kansas City, the 3688 and 3288 were introduced. The 3088 and 3488 Hydro were released later in 1981 with much less fanfare. The 3688, 3288, and 3488 Hydro were tested at the Nebraska Tractor Tests in 1982. Production of the 3488 Hydro was a meager 465 units, the 3088

totaled 1,065 units, and the 3288 closely matched that with 1,162 units. The 3688 led the entire 30 series production with 2,572 units being made. It's very ironic that when the 3088 was finally tested at Nebraska (test #1551) in November of 1984, it would not only be the last tractor tested that year, but also the last IH tractor ever to be tested there.

The "New" IH 60 Series 2+2 Tractors

The IH 60 series 2+2 tractors were proclaimed as the "new feel of power" in IH advertising, but they were really just the original 2+2 series warmed over. The

IH 60 series 2+2 tractor lineup comprised three models: the 130-horsepower model 6388, the 150-horsepower model 6588, and the 170-horsepower model 6788. All three 60 series 2+2s still used the famous IH 400 series six-cylinder turbocharged diesel engines, noted for their industry-leading torque rise, as their power plant.

They were also basically the same as the previous 30 series 2+2 models, except that they now had exterior styling (painting and decals) similar to the 50 and 30 series IH row-crop tractors. The 60 series retained the innovations that made the IH 2+2 tractors the last great

The IH 200 series of tractors. (L to R) Model 254 (21 PTO horsepower), 244 (18 PTO horsepower), 234 hydrostatic-drive and gear-drive (15.2 PTO horsepower) tractors. All of the 200 series were styled to match the larger 50 series tractors. The 200 series tractors were equipped with diesel engines only. *Author Collection*

Delivering 175 PTO horsepower was the model 7288 STS tractor. This tractor had a modified version of the transmission used in the IH 50 series. The PPH hydraulic system, which only operated when needed, saved engine horsepower drain. *Author Collection*

tractor innovation of the millennium. It still used the engine forward and rear cab mounted design for outstanding visibility and weight balance. The IH "Power Priority" hydraulic system, which gave hydraulic priority to the first remote hydraulic outlet, was also retained from the previous models.

One of the major changes that the 60 series 2+2s had over their predecessors were hydraulic-operated transmission brakes. This new style of brake now provided smoother, easier shifting between ranges by positively stopping the transmission gear rotation when the range lever was in neutral and the clutch pedal was depressed. This brake was exactly like what the IH 30 series row-crop gear drive tractors had.

Another change was that the IH 60 series 2+2s had a redesigned Control Center Cab featuring all the controls on the right-hand console, just like in the 30 series row-crop tractors. This left the operator's left hand free for steering. Even though the controls were now located on the right side, a two-door cab

was still offered for easy entry and exit. The IH digital data center was also standard equipment, electronically monitoring several key tractor functions for the operator.

A relatively minor change was in the power steering oil supply pump. IH had some failures and problems with the 30 series 2+2s losing steering pressure or steering hard in the field. Field-testing by the IH Tractor engineering staff showed that a different, more powerful hydraulic supply pump cured the problem.

IH (which was the first manufacturer to equip its tractors from the factory with radial tires) made radial tires standard equipment on the 60 series. This only helped to reiterate the superior traction, flotation, and fuel economy that the IH 2+2 design offered to the farmer. The IH 60 series 2+2s were never tested at Nebraska; instead, they were sold under the test numbers given to the IH 30 series 2+2s. The very volatile U.S. farm economy of the early 1980s, coupled with IH's huge debt load, and serious final drive reliability

problems in the 3788 and 6788, led to a small run of the 60 series 2+2s.

Only 272 of the 6388 tractor, 642 of the 6588 tractor, and 347 of the 6788 tractor were built over their three-year production run from 1981 to 1984. Even today a 60 series IH tractor is a rare find on the farms of North America.

The "New" IH 84 Series Utility/Row-crop Tractors

IH decided to update the reliable 84 row-crop/utility tractor series in 1981. A new 27.4-horsepower model tractor called the 284 diesel joined the 84 series lineup. The 284 diesel had a three-cylinder, water-cooled Nissan diesel engine, which now gave tractor buyers the choice of either a 27.4-horsepower diesel, or 25.8-horsepower gasoline-powered tractor. The addition to the family was the big 84 engine horsepower 884. Like the other models in the 84 series, the 884 offered big tractor features at little tractor prices.

The other major changes to the 84 series were the addition of a FWA axle made by European manufacturer ZF. This heavy-duty axle featured cast-iron construction, greaseable U-joints, and a 42-degree turning angle for tight maneuvering. The right-hand-side driveshaft for the axle had a two-shaft design with a carrier bearing. A crop shield to keep debris from wrapping and a two-door pressurized cab (made by the Sims Mfg. Co.) were optional attachments. The cab attachment was styled to mimic the cab used on the 86 series.

IH now offered three choices of front axles: A swept-back axle for the 484 and 584 allowed a tighter turning radius and reduced steering effort; a tobacco axle extension for all row-crop tractors offered extra ground clearance in tall and bushy plants and helped prevent damage to bedding plants; and a low spindle front axle could be used on the low profile models. This axle lowered the center of gravity and gave greater overhead clearance.

The "lightning flash" arrangement of inline speed gear shifting pattern was replaced by the more conventional and positive H gear-shifting pattern. This made getting the right gear at the right time a lot easier for the operator. A new heavy-duty power-shift TA was offered as standard equipment on the 884 and as an option on the 784 and 684.

A single remote hydraulic valve and lever was standard on all models now, and two valves were still optional. A more responsive steering system reduced the steering effort for even greater maneuverability.

All of the "new" 84 series sported a revised paint and decal scheme. The familiar white wheels and white-painted side panels and trim were replaced by IH red paint, and a thin red pinstripe was added to the tractor's side striping, above the model number and name designation in the same manner as the 1981 model IH 86 series had. This "new" styling helped the revised 84 series look like it was part of the "new" IH family or tractors. All of these "new" IH 84 series still retained the reliable engines, hydraulics, and transmissions the old 84 series offered.

Two models of the old IH 84 series (384 and 484) were replaced by the 383 and 483 tractors, each of which featured four-cylinder water-cooled diesel engines rather than the three-cylinder engines the 384 and 484 had had. The 383 and 483 were produced in Japan and featured such items as: hydrostatic power steering, eight speeds forward, two reverse; optional foot throttle, glow plug-starting diesel engine, differential traction lock, optional ROPS and canopy, and the choice of two- or four-wheel drive.

Little Tractors from Japan

IH contracted with Japanese tractor manufacturer Mitsubishi to produce a new IH compact diesel lineup of tractors. The series comprised three models: the 15-horsepower 234 and 234 Hydro, the 18-horsepower 244, and the 21-horsepower 254. They were styled to look similar to their bigger IH 50 series tractor brothers.

Using three-cylinder overhead-valve liquid-cooled diesel engines, the 200 series was a group of power-packed compact tractors. The use of an electric fuel shutoff solenoid kept the tractor from

The big brother to the 7288 is the 200 PTO horsepower model 7488 STS tractor. The 7488 could be equipped with dual wheels (both front and rear) for added traction and flotation. The 7488 never went into full production, with only 16 units being built before the series was mothballed. *Author Collection*

"dieseling" after the ignition was switched off. All members of the 200 series were equipped with vertical exhaust mufflers, which could be turned to a horizontal position to gain extra overhead clearance. The fully enclosed engine featured a forward tip-off hood and quick-release side panels. It was also easy to check the engine oil level, thanks to an opening in the side panel that allowed quick access to the engine oil dipstick. A slide-out screen allowed the operator to clean out any debris that might plug the radiator. The battery was located ahead of the radiator for easy maintenance and cleaning access. A dry-type air filter element trapped 99 percent of air contaminants before they reached the engine. Basic engine maintenance was easy, too, since the lubricating oil filter and diesel fuel filter were both spin-on types.

Shift levers were floor-mounted on gear-drive models. A nine-speed gear-drive transmission (244 and 254) featured speeds from .80 mph up to 12.6 mph. The 234 gear-drive featured six speeds, and the Hydrostatic 234, which used a hand-operated lever beside the instrument panel for finger-touch control, had a 0 to 9.6-mph speed range. Other features included a transmission oil-level dipstick located to the left of the shift lever, and a standard rear differential lock on all models that gave wheels sure traction. The 244 and 254 featured a dual speed (540 and 1,250 rpm) PTO. The 234 had a 540-rpm rear PTO and an electrically engaged 2,700-rpm front-mounted PTO.

The 200 series also offered a complete lighting package: Two large combination amber flashing lights and turn signals, along with dual recessed front headlights, made work more productive and safer. An optional rear fender–mounted work light was also available.

For operator comfort, the high-backed padded seat offered three height position choices to fit any operator. Directly below the seat was a handy tool storage box.

All three models had optional FWA and a choice of either AG or turf-style tires. The 244 and 254 each could be equipped with optional synchronized transmission with live rear PTO, while the 234 offered an optional independent front PTO. Power steering could be added to the 244 and 254, if desired. All three tractors were well suited for larger estate care duties and came with a wide choice of attachments: Mowers, plows, disk harrows, front loaders, and blades and much more. Each tractor was equipped with a category I three-point rear hitch and a two-post ROPS. A canopy shade top was optional equipment.

IH Creates a New Marketing Approach

Farmers were not buying much, if any machinery at all, with depressed commodity markets, high interest rates, and lower exports in the early 1980s. Thousands of farms in the United States were being lost every month. This great decline in rural businesses caused the government to take action and help the farmer. Two programs were immediately developed, one of which was called the CRP (Conservation Reserve Program), which paid farmers to leave idle highly erodible cropland for a period of 10 years with the idea that removing some land from the crop production base would hopefully bolster commodity prices. The other program was called the PIK, or Payment In Kind program. Basically, farmers would be paid with commodity price certificates for their crops, to help support their income.

IH used the PIK program in 1983 to offer farmers its "Crop Swap" program. This unique method of marketing allowed IH dealers to accept PIK certificates as trade collateral on new IH machinery. A special "Crop Swap" telephone hotline was established to give IH dealers up-to-the-minute commodity price information. For the farmer it meant the possibility of "trading" PIK certificates for partial payment on new IH machinery instead of using cash. This would allow the farmer to still take advantage of both the investment tax credit and machinery depreciation allowance. This did help some IH dealers move iron in the worst of economic times and help to keep their doors open.

The Last "New" IH Tractors: The 7288 and 7488 STS

In 1979 with machine tooling dollars already becoming very tight, and financial ruin just around the corner, IH started to design a tractor series that would replace the current 2+2 series and set the stage for IH's re-entry into the 200 horsepower and larger four-wheel-drive market. The company planned to save thousands of dollars in tooling costs by using the TR4 (50 series) drivetrain in a slightly modified form. The primary objective of this new series was to provide a tractor with maximum productivity in tillage and row-crop use. The engine forward- and rear-mounted control center, like that on the previous 2+2 series, was retained for this tractor series. Nearly 100,000 hours of component, powertrain, and tractor testing were performed prior to the start of this new tractor's production.

With the higher horsepower capability of the 50 series transmission, IH could re-enter the 200 horsepower and above four-wheel-drive market. The old 2+2 design of driving the front axle from the transmission countershaft via a side-mounted gearbox could be eliminated. The 50 series was designed with a centerline driveshaft option to run a powered front axle. A new center transfer case and articulation joint was designed to handle the higher horsepower loads and stresses these tractors would have to withstand.

A new 4-inch diameter bar-type front axle rated at 100 horsepower provided the necessary capacities for a wide range of uses. The RABA Company (from Hungary) built this new axle. RABA also built drive axles for the Steiger Tractor Co., of Fargo, North Dakota for use in its four-wheel-drive tractors. The axle could easily absorb the stresses of maximum loading that could be imposed when the tractor was equipped with dual 300-gallon front-mounted chemical tanks. The tractor's wheelbase was extended 6 inches to allow the use of dual wheels on both the front and rear without any tire interference when turning. A unique feature of the axle was its built-in oil cooling capability: An internal heat exchanger dissipated the heat of the axle oil by circulating oil through it from the transmission oil cooler. This oil was then returned to the transmission and recirculated again with the transmission oil.

IH wanted these new four-wheel drives to be the best they had ever made. The hydraulic system from the 50 series was beefed up to provide a combined pumping capacity of over 86 gallons per minute! Three hydraulic pumps constituted the basic system. All three were externally mounted on the right side of the transmission for easy service, should that be needed. Because of high flow and pressure requirements for four-wheel-drive tractor steering, a flow compensated piston-type hydraulic pump—dedicated to the steering function only—was used. The three-point hitch was beefed up, and now had a lifting capacity of more than 9,890 pounds! Heavy-duty lower hitch link arms and top links were used, too. IH was dead serious about building the premier four-wheel-drive row-crop tractor.

The original hand-built prototype was made using the transmission/final drive from a 1982 model 5288. IH's plans originally called for two models to be built in this series, a 235-horsepower model 7488 and a 250-horsepower model 7688. However, the 7688 model was dropped and replaced with a lower horsepower 7288 even before a prototype 7688 could be built. Both of the Super 70 series four-wheel drives used the reliable IH-built DTI466C engines. These inline six-cylinder turbocharged and intercooled engines produced 210 horsepower for the 7288 and a whopping 235 horsepower for the 7488.

In a product price bulletin dated August 20, 1984, IH stated: "September 4, 1984, will mark the start of production

This 7488 easily handles its trailing IH moldboard plow at the IH Hickory Hills testing farm near Seneca, Illinois. With the Super 70 series lineup introduction scheduled for August 1984, IH photographers were busy at Hickory Hills in June shooting literature photos. *Author Collection*

7088, 7288, and 7488 PTO Horsepower Ratings			
Model	**Engine**	**Test No.**	**PTO Power**
7088	DT-436B Diesel	Never built	150
7288	DTI-466C Diesel	No test	175
7488	DTI-466C Diesel	No test	200

of the all new International 70 series four wheel drive tractors. These units will satisfy the customer's demands for increased horsepower and versatility, which would allow them to better utilize their investment dollars through increased hour utilization. The new 210 and 235 engine horsepower 70 series incorporate: an improved 50 series power train, increased hydraulic and hitch capacities, improved steering ease and the reliability your customers expect in a four wheel drive tractor."

One interesting note is the chrome exhaust pipe that adorns the Super 70 tractors shown in the sales literature. This was a $25 option from IH, but nearly every surviving Super 70 has one on it. When IH sold its agricultural equipment division to Tenneco, this prompted the termination of the Super 70 series four-wheel drives. Of the 150 tractors to be built in the pilot production run, only 35 models survive. At the time of the sale, the 7288 hand-built prototype was left at the IH Proving Grounds in Phoenix, Arizona, and later purchased by an IH dealer nearby. The first 7488 also spent time at the Phoenix Proving Grounds. However, it was parked at the Nebraska Tractor Test Center in Lincoln awaiting its turn to be tested when the sale of IH's Ag Equipment Division was announced. No one at Lincoln knew what to do with the 7488, so it stayed there a few months. Finally, a machinery jockey from Grand Meadow, Minnesota, bought the 7488 and resold it to a farmer near Waukee, Iowa.

A number of the Super 70s that were still on the assembly line, or had not left the Farmall Works, were destroyed on site. A quick nip of the cutting torch to the diesel engine's fuel-injection pump and the tractor was officially "scrapped." Many of the parts used for the tractor's assembly were treated in the same man-

ner. There was about half a semi-truck load of the polished chrome exhaust stacks in the plant that were determined to be "nonessential," and crushed and sold for scrap price. Too bad someone didn't realize that those chrome pipes would also fit the 50 series tractors. Most of the production tooling was either scrapped or mothballed for future use.

A number of the service repair parts for the Super 70 series today are listed as "unique parts for 70 series prototype machines & will not be supplied when present inventory is depleted." To the owner of one of these tractors today, that translates into "find a good machine shop and try not to wreck it too bad."

Another orphan Super 70 series tractor was planned to be released by IH in 1985. This model was designated the 7088 and was to be the 150-horsepower replacement for the 3588 and 6588, the most popular 2+2 model.

The base list price in 1984 for the 7288 was $83,631, and the 7488 was $90,101, both when equipped with standard equipment only. A few of the Super 70s did find homes in farmers' sheds. IH only sold 35 tractors total, 19 7288s and 16 were 7488s. These tractors are instant modern-day IH collectibles, with many still bringing over $60,000— that is, if you can even find one for sale.

The IH 2+2 Recall That Never Happened

In the early 1980s, IH management was wrestling internally to get the new TR4 transmission included in the next 2+2 when the 50 series was announced. Delays and cost overruns postponed this event until the Super 70 series was announced in 1984. IH was deathly afraid that the old 2+2 stigma would be applied to the new Super 70 series tractors. It wanted to reestablish the image of the

2+2, head off any competitive reaction, and finally increase IH sales and market share. To overcome any doubts about IH's commitment to the 2+2 design, a 2+2-tractor recall program was devised.

IH had planned for owners of all 3388, 3588, and 3788 2+2 tractors to have their machines hauled to the Farmall Works in Rock Island for a "rebuild." This "rebuild" program would cost the owner of a 3388 and 3588 a $500 fee. Owners of 3788s would pay a $1,000 fee. For this "fee" the IH dealer would pay to have the tractor transported to and from Farmall, while IH would pay for the installation of the necessary rebuild kit to be installed. IH estimated the cost of this "rebuild" program to be $11.4 million for the 5,224 tractors that were affected.

The program would involve replacing the transmission brake with an electric brake and electric shift TA on all 2+2s. These features were included on the 60 series 2+2s. On the 3388 and 3588, IH planned to add the following new components: Heavy Duty TA, rear countershaft, wiring harness, clutch and pressure plate, axle bearings and seals; it would also renew the articulation bearing and sleeve, install new hood latches, inspect the fuel tank baffle, check and update the air-conditioning system, and replace the closed center hydraulic system with an open center system. The 3788 would also have the aforementioned items replaced along with the replacement of the differential (ring gear and pinion). All of this was to be done while the tractor was at Farmall.

IH also planned to update the 60 series 2+2s in the field, with kits installed by the local IH dealer. The 60 series update was to include change to the hydraulic system to open center and the addition of auxiliary hood latches.

The 2+2 rebuild program was to be announced to dealers at a special "Red Power" show to be held in November 1984, at the IH Engineering Center in Hinsdale. After the rebuild was performed on customers, 2+2s, a special gold rebuild plate would be installed on the tractor. This plate would list the customer's name, date of rebuild, and factory seal of installation. A follow-up thank-you letter would be sent to the customer. The IH 2+2 rebuild program was to start October 1, 1984, and be finished by April 1, 1985.

The End of an Era . . .
The Final Farmall-built Tractor

The announcement of IH's sale of its Ag Equipment division was one that rippled through the industry. In future years ahead, many former competitors of IH would meet the same fate. It was decided to rationalize the manufacturing overcapacity of the tractor industry. The old and largely antiquated facility of the Farmall Works was just too expensive to operate efficiently in a declining marketplace. Tractor production at Farmall was to be dropped in early 1985. Plans were made to slowly phase out tractor production and workers over a six-month period. Many of the production tools were relocated to other manufacturing plants for future use.

On April 3, 1985, the final Farmall-built tractor (5488 AWD) started down the assembly line. The transmission/final drive assembly was set on the main assembly line for the final leg of its historic journey. On April 5, the engine, frame rails, and FWA axle were added to the rear transmission/final drive housing. April 9 saw the Forward Air-Flow cooling system air box and engine radiator join the assembly. On the April 10, the tractor's chassis was painted IH black and the operator's platform was added. Some idle assembly time passed, as the tractor's Control Center Cab was not added until May 1, at which time the hood panels, decal striping, and deep treaded "rice-style" tires were also done.

Finally, on May 14, 1985, the end came. In a very small ceremony among only a handful of reporters (and with very little fanfare), the final Farmall tractor was rolled off the assembly line. Photos were taken and speeches were given, but this was the end of the line for Farmall. After producing 2,084,859 IH tractors for 40 years, the Farmall Works closed. The 5488 FWA

The end of an era. The final Farmall-built tractor, a model 5488 with FWA. This 5488 started on the assembly line in April of 1985 and was finished on May 14, 1985. It signaled not only the closing of the Farmall plant, but it was also the last IH 50 series tractor built. The 5488 is owned by Case Corporation and is currently in storage in Racine, Wisconsin. *Author Collection*

SN#2590009U004552 rolled into IH tractor history, just like the Farmall Works itself.

A special leaflet was printed in 1986 commemorating the milestones in the Farmall Works history. Inside this leaflet are photos of the 16 IH tractor murals inside Farmall. These paintings were hand-painted on the assembly line wall of the plant by former employee Mary Ramsey, and still survive intact today. Several Farmall Works production milestones are listed in this "obituary" too.

An example is from the summer of 1955, when Farmall produced 325 tractors in one day. That is about 13.5 tractors per hour, or one tractor built every 4 minutes. (That is faster than any auto quick lube!) Another example occurred on December 5, 1979, when the Farmall Works produced its 2 millionth tractor (a 1086), a manufacturing milestone that was only recently met by its competitor (Deere), nearly 20 years later. The plant officially closed on June 30, 1986.

Index

Ag Equipment Division, 126, 127
Air Maze Company, 67
Anderson, Andy, 22
Behlen Mfg. Co., 9
Bostic, Jim, 109
Brass Tacks, 17, 20, 34, 35
Campbell, Rich, 78
Case Corporation, 127
Coleman Manufacturing Co., 43, 68
Commercial Shearing Pump Co., 119
Conservation Reserve Program (CRP), 124
Control Center Cab, 86, 88, 113, 115, 122, 127
Deluxe Fenders, 48
Deutz, 119
Direct Drive, 13
Dyna-Life, 67
Electrall, 12, 14-16
Elwood Mfg., 115
Engineering Test Center, 81, 83, 86, 114, 116, 119, 126
ERTL Company, 78, 100
Excel Co., 61
Farmall Plant, 83
Farmall Works, 48, 102, 126, 127
Fast Hitch, 9-11, 13-16, 21, 25, 26, 29, 35, 40, 42, 48, 82
Fast Reverser, 25
Ferguson, Harry, 13
Fordson, 53
Forward Air Flow, 112, 113, 115
Frame-All, 14
Frank Hough Industrial Division, 79
Froelich, 53
Full Powershift, 116
Gold Demonstrator Tractor Program, 63, 64
Hickory Hills, 125
Hough Industrial Division, 31, 51
IH 806 pedal tractor, 36
John Deere, 33, 36, 90, 107, 114
Johnson, Shirley, 114
Johnson, Stuart, 114, 116
Kittleson, Lowell, 33
Martinson Implement, 115
Massey-Ferguson, 73, 81
McAllister, 83
McLaughlin Manufacturing Company, 69
Midway Equipment Co., 50
Mississippi Road Supply (MRS), 79
Mitsubishi, 123
Multiple Control Valve (MCV), 39
Museum of History and Technology, 53
Nerroth, Barbara, 52
Nerroth, Greg, 52
New World of Power, 34
Otter, Harry, 58
Otters Sales & Service, 58
Payment in Kind (PIK), 124
Phoenix Proving Grounds, 126
Pilot Guide, 16
Power Priority system, 98, 99, 102, 103, 113, 120
PTO, 42
RABA Company, 124

Ramsey, Mary, 127
Reverse Airflow (R-A-F), 113
Roll-over protective structure (ROPS), 45, 64, 67, 69, 75, 84, 85, 123, 124
Rosa Master, 37, 38, 42, 57
Selecto-Speed, 25
Sentry, 110, 115
Sims Mfg. Co., 122
Smithsonian Institution, 53
SOLAR division, 46
Speed Ratio, 51
Steiger Tractor Co., 63, 79, 80, 81, 84, 114, 116, 119, 124
Stockton Works, 32
Stolper-Allen, 45
Synchro Tri-Six (STS), 110, 111, 114
Tenneco, 126
Torque Amplifier (TA), 11, 26, 28, 36, 39, 48, 54, 67, 68, 85, 86, 120, 126
Touch Control system, 9, 11
Traction Control, 14
Vari-Torque, 115, 116

Models
00 Series, 10
06 Series, 40, 42, 57-59, 68
1500 Series, 84
2+2 Series, 97-100, 126, 127
26 Series, 55
30 Series, 119-121
30 Series 2+2, 121
50 Series, 16, 109-116, 124, 126
54 Series, 64, 65
56 Series, 55, 59, 68
60 Series 2+2, 121, 122
66 Series, 58, 67-69, 72, 74, 75, 85, 86, 90, 93
68 Series, 74
70 Series, 119
74 Series, 64-66
84 Series, 91, 93, 109, 122, 123
86 Series, 42, 82, 83, 91, 94, 101-103
86 Series Pro Ag Line, 78, 86-90, 92, 93
200 Series, 121, 123, 124
300 Series, 71
400 Series, 71
Cub, 15, 17, 23, 35
Cub Cadet, 29, 102
Cub Cadet Original, 36
Cub Lo-Boy, 14, 20, 23, 35
Farmall Cub, 10
Magnum 7100 Series, 116
Model 2+2, 101, 104-107
Model 100, 9-11
Model 123 Cub Cadet, 55
Model 130, 15-17
Model 140, 9, 19, 20, 23, 35
Model 186 Hydro, 86, 89
Model 200, 9, 10
Model 230, 15-17
Model 234, 109, 121, 123
Model 234 Hydro, 123
Model 240, 20-23, 25, 35
Model 244, 109, 121, 124
Model 250, 21

Model 254, 109, 121, 123, 124
Model 274, 120
Model 284, 122
Model 300, 9-11, 33
Model 330, 16
Model 340, 21-23, 25, 35, 51-53
Model 340 Grove, 22
Model 350, 15-17, 33
Model 354, 64, 66, 75
Model 360, 28, 29
Model 383, 109, 123
Model 384, 91, 123
Model 400, 9-13, 17, 21, 33
Model 404, 30, 31, 36, 37
Model 450, 15-18, 20, 33
Model 454, 64, 66, 67, 75
Model 460, 23-29, 32-35, 37
Model 460 Grove, 27, 28
Model 460 Hi-Utility, 26, 27
Model 460 Orchard, 27
Model 460 Wheat Land, 26, 27
Model 483, 109, 123
Model 484, 91, 101, 122, 123
Model 504, 27, 34, 36, 37
Model 544, 53, 54, 56, 57, 63, 64
Model 560, 22-29, 32-35
Model 560 Brass Tacks demonstrator, 33
Model 574, 64, 66-68
Model 584, 91, 122
Model 606, 37
Model 650, 17
Model 656, 36, 43, 49, 50, 53, 55, 57, 63, 64
Model 656 Hydro, 50
Model 660, 24, 28, 35
Model 664, 65-67
Model 666, 53, 81-83
Model 674, 66, 67
Model 684, 91, 123
Model 686, 83, 86, 97
Model 706, 36-46, 49, 50
Model 756, 53, 55, 59, 61, 63
Model 766, 67-69, 73, 75, 86, 88
Model 784, 91, 123
Model 786, 89, 107
Model 806, 36-46, 48-50
Model 826, 53, 54, 63, 64
Model 856, 55, 58, 59, 61
Model 856 Wheat Land, 55
Model 884, 123
Model 886, 86, 89, 92, 101, 107
Model 966, 67-69, 72, 74, 75, 77, 86
Model 986, 86, 89, 92, 107
Model 1026, 48, 53, 54, 63, 64
Model 1066, 67, 68, 70, 71, 74, 75-78, 83, 86, 88
Model 1066 Hydro, 75, 76
Model 1066 Turbo, 75, 88
Model 1068, 73
Model 1086, 86, 89, 92, 93, 95, 96, 100, 107
Model 1155, 73
Model 1206, 45, 58, 61
Model 1206 Turbo, 43, 46, 48-51
Model 1206 Turbo prototype, 41
Model 1256, 55, 59, 61
Model 1456, 59, 61, 63, 64

Model 1466, 67-69, 72, 74, 75, 79-81, 86
Model 1468, 67, 68, 73, 74, 81, 82
Model 1482 Axial Flow combine, 96, 118, 119
Model 1486, 86, 89, 92, 107
Model 1566, 84, 85, 87, 91
Model 1568, 84, 85
Model 1586, 86, 89, 92, 94, 101, 107
Model 3088, 108, 109, 120, 121
Model 3288, 109, 120, 121
Model 3388, 97, 126
Model 3488, 120, 121
Model 3488 Hydro, 116
Model 3588, 97, 100, 101, 126
Model 3688, 108, 109, 120, 121
Model 3788, 97, 100, 126
Model 4000, 61
Model 4100, 44-46, 51
Model 4156, 51, 71
Model 4166, 71, 78-80
Model 4168, 79
Model 4266, 79
Model 4300, 31, 32, 51
Model 4366, 79-81, 84
Model 4386, 63, 90, 99
Model 4468, 79
Model 4500 field cultivator, 117
Model 4568, 81, 84
Model 4586, 90, 98
Model 4786, 90
Model 5000, 114
Model 5088, 108-111, 113-115
Model 5188, 114, 115, 116
Model 5288, 108-111, 113-115, 124
Model 5488, 108-111, 113-115, 127
Model 6388, 109, 121, 122
Model 6588, 109, 121, 122
Model 6588 2+2, 117-119
Model 6788, 109, 121
Model 7088, 126
Model 7288, 124, 126
Model 7288 STS, 122
Model 7388, 109, 114, 116, 119
Model 7488, 124-126
Model 7488 JTS, 123
Model 7588, 109, 116, 119
Model 7688, 124
Model 7788, 109, 116, 119
Model HT-340, 47
Model Hydro 70, 85, 89
Model Hydro 84, 91
Model Hydro 86, 86
Model Hydro 100, 85, 88
Model Hydro 186, 92
Model M, 17
Model Taco Special, 107
Model TX 202, 119
Model TX 203, 119
Model TX 204, 119
Model TX 96 II prototype, 83
Model TX189, 115, 116
Power Priority Hydraulics (PPH) series, 89
Super 70 Series, 126
Super MTA, 33
Super W6TA, 33
Tri Stripe 86 Series, 99, 102, 103